Boom and Bust
Killing the American Dream

Mike Crane & Matt Grubesic

ISBN:1533409099
ISBN-13:9781533409096

DEDICATION

To those millions who went before us and created the American Dream, and to those who still believe in it.

Also by This Author:

Vengeance: a Novel of the Viet Nam War
Parallel Lives

CONTENTS

ACKNOWLEDGMENTS

Neither of us could have completed this work without the help
of those honest people who taught us in our youth, and
demanded we think clearly and objectively. They were too few
and far between.

Boom and Bust

Killing the American Dream

Lady Liberty is sinking. Jobs disappear overseas, never to return. Those lucky enough not to have lost their homes to foreclosure (or being forced by unemployment to hand them back to the bank, which is nevertheless a disappearing option) often can't move even if they wanted to: like Lady Liberty, they're "under water." In other words, they owe more on the house than they can get for it on the market.

Almost sounds like the country as a whole...

Many young people are stuck in dead-end jobs. Others pile up huge balances on college loans in the hopes of a better tomorrow...

Old people wonder whether Social Security will be around for much longer. People approaching retirement age wonder the same thing, but for slightly different reasons.

And still other Americans, those in the middle years, struggle to get ahead, to buy a house, to save anything at all.

The American Dream is dying. More Americans say the country is on the wrong track than those who think otherwise. And personal liberty itself fades away, a shimmering ideal from a long-lost past.

We hear it again, over and over. "America is bankrupt." "The middle class is dying." "The country is on the wrong track."

We hear all these things and more. There seems little doubt that middle-class America has taken some hits in the last eight years. The picture in Anytown, USA looks grim sometimes.

What the hell happened?!

One

Anytown, USA: Today

The young man walked into his apartment, snarling angrily to himself. Obviously, his experiences with the bank had been distasteful. He looked up, a surprise visitor catching his attention from the corner of his eye.

"Hey, Dad. I didn't know you were coming by."

The older man held up his cell phone.

"Glories of twenty-first-century technology," he grinned. "Got a text message," he added, when his son's face didn't twist into a smile.

"Good to see you. I could use someone to talk to."

"What's the matter, son?" the older man asked.

"It's the damned bank, Dad. They won't give us the loan to buy that house Mary Jane and I wanted. It seems that our income isn't high enough."

"But you both work..."

"I know, and the bank knows it, too. Even still, though we're both earning good money, we can't cut it. Hell, a family has to have two incomes just to stay ahead of the game anymore. We aren't even doing as well as you are, Dad, and both of us work. We aren't even doing as well as you were when you and Mom were our age!"

"Funny to hear you say that, son. I had a conversation with *my* dad about that very same thing." The older man looked out the window wistfully. "Can't believe it's been thirty years..." he added.

"You and Grandpa talked about this, too?"

The younger man's frustration rose.

"How in the..." he began, then caught himself as he saw his young daughter playing in the next room. Suppressing his instinct for locker-room language between himself and his father, he continued. "... world could that be the case? You guys did so much better than we're doing."

"I know it seems that way, son. But things just aren't that clear-cut. We sure *thought* we were doing well. I compared notes with your grandfather when I was about your age. And was just about as frustrated, too, I might add."

The younger man walked over to the couch and sat down. His father leaned back in the leather chair he'd given his son a few years ago, which had once sat in his own father's living room, settling in for a long conversation.

"I could stand some good news, Dad. Not sure this counts, but..."

"It's true, son. We Baby Boomers thought life was going to be easy, and when most of us hit thirty or so, and we looked around, we thought the cards were stacked against us. All we remembered, it seemed, was how well our parents did. We sort of ignored the Great Depression."

"I remember Grandpa talking about that when I was little. Must have been a big deal."

"It was. A life-forming experience, you could say."

"How long did it last?"

"You're not going to pester me for 'official' dates, are you?" the older man laughed. "You sound like your friend, the engineer. There aren't any such dates."

The younger man scowled, knowing that his father was right, and waited for the answer he knew would follow.

"In October, 1929, the stock market crashed. But the Depression didn't start the next day. What followed was a sort of series of cascading effects as one after another things happened, and within a few months, things were tough. Really tough. High unemployment. And to make things worse, land speculators in the Midwest lost their shirts when the weather turned over a period of years, and created the 'Dust Bowl' about the same time."

"I never heard about that."

"Starving farmers aren't as sexy as stock brokers throwing themselves off the Empire State Building, son," the older man intoned ruefully. "But you can find lots of pictures on the Internet."

The younger man resisted the urge to pull his smartphone out of his pocket, knowing he could look later. As always, his father had piqued his interest.

"So when did it end?"

"People say the Second World War ended it. But they mean when America entered the war in December, 1941. That isn't really true, but that's how people think about it."

"So more than ten years? The Depression lasted more than ten years?"

"Yes. Imagine being a little kid, like your grandfather, for that whole time. So you can understand his thinking a lot better."

"Some people have been saying these times are the worst since then, like voters know about the Depression."

"These times are worse, but for different reasons."

The younger man's face flashed confusion as his father's words sank in.

How can what's happening now be worse than that? he thought to himself.

"Tell me what happened after the war, Dad."

"Men who fought the war came home. The way I taught the subject in class was that their minds were changed. They'd grown up during the Depression, then they'd fought and won World War II, and it was as if they just decided, as a group, to work their tails off and make a better world so that my generation wouldn't have either of those problems, ever again."

"Grandpa worked hard, didn't he?"

"I didn't see him much when I was little," the father replied. "He worked sixty hours a week, or more, pretty often. And all year 'round."

"But you made more than he did, didn't you? At the same age, I mean. I remember you telling me that once."

"If you mean accounting for inflation and all that, yes. Dad got a little GI Bill house in the fifties and we lived in that for years. Mom stayed home with us because we liked it that way. All of us, I mean: my sister and I, and Dad and Mom, too."

"So what happened? Why did you think you were worse off than your folks?"

"Our vision changed. I've thought about this a lot. Every man wants his son to do better than *he* did, right? At least any man worth being called a man. But what you don't often hear is that sons generally want to outdo their dads, too. I did. And whether you know it or not, you do, too."

The son looked at the floor for a second, slightly embarrassed at being caught in what he thought was his Big Secret. Then he looked back up, seeing his father smiling.

"Yeah, it's true. At least for me," the younger man replied.

"And it seemed like the Boomers were living up to that."

The son watched his father as he spoke. The older man's fingers came up one after another, as if he were ticking off a bullet-list in his head.

"Everyday things required less work-time to earn them. And we had better cars," the father continued. "Air-conditioned houses, and more of them. For you it's cell phones; for us it was VCRs and so-called 'home computers.' More people went to college. In fact, what with our parents pushing us, and a lot of Boomers going to college so they could stay out of Vietnam, my generation pretty much made higher education the national sport."

"No kidding. High school won't get you anywhere anymore."

"That's a different problem for a different day, son," the old man chuckled. "And for the record," he smiled," I don't fully agree. But a hundred years ago, only six per cent of adults had a high-school diploma. And a hundred and fifty years ago, graduating the eighth grade in some places required a knowledge of the Constitution that my grad-school profs would have been hard-pressed to answer."

"So you were better off materially than Grandpa's generation?"

"Yes, we were. We just didn't see it. And a lot of people complained about that, believe it or not, back in the sixties. When they were being polite, they'd call us 'insensitive materialists.' Those of us chasing a better life, that is. And I guess that was true to some degree. But if those same people had known any history at all, they'd have known that the march of Western civilization has largely been one based on economic desires."

"Is that how you put it in class, dad?"

The old man nodded as he continued.

"Yes. Materialism has been a preoccupation of the masses forever. As some smart-alecks claimed about the 'progress' of the French Revolution, the peasants had seized the 'freedom' to starve to death. Obviously, those people thought that central control was better than freedom and liberty. Hard to believe it was Americans saying that. But let's get back to your question. You know how I can be when you get me talking history."

The younger man smiled at the gleam in his father's eye. Indeed, the son knew, and redirected.

"So you wanted more and sooner than Grandpa's generation did."

"That might be the understatement of the year. Boomers had more income, more possessions, more education, and more wealth than their parents. They didn't need two incomes to have what their parents had. Sometimes, however, because of increased expectations, we wanted both spouses to work so that we could have the things that we remember having as children. But we forgot about how our folks had to pay their dues. So, yes: we had higher expectations, and I sometimes think we passed that on to our kids."

The son redirected yet again.

"I guess it all comes down to what your bench-mark is."

"Spoken like a true businessman," the father smiled. "But you face problems now that we didn't face thirty years ago."

"Like what?"

"We had growing government, but not like now. We had pundits on television telling us what to think, but not like the big-mouthed ones we have now. And a lot of people thought government had the solutions to their problems, but not as much as now. Of course there was that whole 'Dewey defeats Truman' thing."

"What?"

"You think pollsters and people predicting the future is a twenty-first-century thing, son? There were all sorts of people doing that when I was a kid, and even before I was born. Probably the most famous instance was when a newspaper went with the prediction that Thomas Dewey was going to beat Harry Truman in the 1948 Presidential election."

"Who's Thomas Dewey?"

"My point exactly... And now the outcomes of elections are predicted before the elections even commence. It's big business, telling the future. But at some point, predicting the future ends up being self-fulfilling."

Recently re-elected President, Harry S Truman, gleefully holds up a front-page newspaper article announcing his defeat. Pollsters had determined Truman's opponent, Thomas Dewey, would win, and the newspaper went with that story before the actual outcome was known.

"But people were more honest back then, weren't they?"

"Not really, son. Corruption then, and corruption now. The joke back then, one of them, at any rate, was about 'welfare Cadillacs.'"

"Welfare Cadillacs?!"

"Yes. Exactly that. Some woman got caught collecting multiple welfare checks under as many names. She'd been doing it for years, and it took practically forever for her to get caught. But the point was, she drove a Cadillac, the biggest-status car back then. A guy named Jerry Reed even sang a song that went to the top of the charts."

"About welfare Cadillacs?"

"No, not exactly. But one of the lines at the end of the song, when he was going to jail, was, 'Who's gonna collect my welfare? Pay for my Cadillac?'"

The younger man laughed.

"They're more sophisticated now."

"Maybe, son. I'd say it's more a matter of degree than of kind. Besides, young people always think they know more than those who went before."

The son scowled.

"I didn't say *all* young people, son. And I wasn't exempting my generation, either. We behaved the same way, especially in the sixties. Maybe worse."

"So about that degree-and-kind thing..."

"Well, computer fraud is more sophisticated than paper fraud, one could argue," the older man answered. "But it's still fraud. It's the same kind of thing. Lots of examples in the world of things being the same kind of thing as what we've always done, but now done to a different degree."

"OK, got it. But back to the problems we have now that are worse than during the Great Depression..."

"The elites are stealing from you."

"Whoa... Dad, that's pretty wild talk."

The son looked at his father closely, studying his face for the faintest hint of a smile. The older man could tell jokes in a completely dead-pan manner, and say the most outlandish things with the straightest of faces. As a boy, his father had joked with him that way, and sometimes more than the older man should have, without meaning to.

Not the faintest hint of a smile crept across the older man's face.

"You're serious, aren't you?"

"I've never been more serious in my life, son."

"But you said..."

"I said what I meant, and I meant what I said. The elites are stealing from you. Stealing your capital. Stealing your wealth. And stealing your freedom while they do it."

"I'm not sure I want to hear this, but I'm pretty sure I *need* to hear this."

"You know things work in cycles, right?"

"Everything, dad. Business cycles, cycles in nature... Yeah, everything."

"Ever heard of 'boom and bust?'"

"Once in a general-ed class I had to take. The prof talked about it like we knew what it was..."

"And no one cared enough to ask?"

"No," the son replied sheepishly.

The older man let the lesson teach itself, rather than tell his son yet again that there is no such thing as a stupid question, except the unasked question.

"A boom-and-bust cycle is an exaggerated business cycle. When a hot new product comes out, the price is high. That's the upswing. In a few years, or sometimes even just a few months, suppliers rush to get in on the good market, and then the market gets saturated, and prices come down. And some of those suppliers go out of business because they got over-extended in their lust for more and more sales, as if the high prices would last forever."

"And a boom-and-bust cycle is worse?"

"Yes. You remember the tech boom in the late 90s."

"I was still young..."

"And compared to me, you still are," the father laughed. "But you heard about it."

"Yes."

"Everyone was convinced that the Internet was the solution to all things. It was the wave of the future."

"But ... it was..." the son interjected.

"Of course it was the wave of the future. Just like railroads in the nineteenth century. But what people did was bid the prices of tech stocks higher and higher, and eventually the market simply wouldn't bear higher prices, and when the sell-offs began, a lot of people lost their money, because they'd gone into debt to buy more and more tech stocks."

"Didn't..." the son began, then his voice trailed off.

"Didn't that happen with radio stocks in the 1920s? Yes."

"Sort of a different degree, but the same kind," the son smiled.

"Exactly. People back then were buying on margin with no collateral at all. They were buying stocks for ten cents on the dollar. And that was fine as long as the stocks went up. And when those prices went down, the margin-buyers couldn't pay their debts because they had no money in the bank, so they sold as fast as they could, which only pushed prices down farther and faster."

"I don't hear people in the media saying 'boom-and-bust,' though."

"Boom-and-bust, as an expression, fell out of favor after the Depression. People like to change the names of things, especially when the things the names of which they want to change scare the hell out of them. So a 'bust' is now called a 'shakeout' or a 'market correction,' as if those candy-coated names somehow lessen the pain."

"And that thing with the sell-offs... That's one of the spiraling effects you were talking about a minute ago."

"Right. And so now you see: cycles can turn into boom-and-bust cycles if too many people get too over-extended."

"Sorta like now, with houses... And you lived in a boom era, and now we're having the bust?"

"You've got it, son. The trouble is, there's more to the story. This isn't just the natural cycle at work. Like I said, the elites are stealing your capital. Stealing it now like they never could before."

* * * *

Fantasy? Hardly. Let us examine the actual situation, exemplified by the case of the young man who believes his father lived better than he does.

Two

Capital and Third-Party Payers

Over the last 250 years the United States has grown into a huge, integrated, industrialized system that makes up over a quarter of the world economy. We must ask ourselves: why did this occur here in America, and nowhere else in the world? This phenomenon occurred in the United States because of the Founding Fathers' vision: their establishment of the Constitution; property rights (both real and intellectual); a government that protected the freedoms of the majority and the rights of the minority; and most importantly, established limited government.

Consequently, entrepreneurship, discovery, and a market economy resulted, allowing consumers to make their own choices and accumulate capital. This last piece is critical.

What is capital? This critical term is often misunderstood. Is capital money? No: money is a medium of exchange when making a transaction, a measure of value or a payment. Beer was a form of payment at one time. For example, the Mesopotamians were paid in beer for their labor. Roman soldiers were paid in salt.

One kind of capital is human. Adam Smith described human capital and was instrumental in creating the public-school system in America. Educated people are an asset to a society, and most become productive, innovative, self-relying members contributing to the economy. An educated person is the foundation for economic development and a higher standard of living for all.

Natural resources used for the production of goods and services are another form of capital. The machinery created for the farmer to plant his crops on land, which produces food for everyone is yet another type. All of those components contributing to production and the end result (in this case, soybeans) are capital. The machinery made by private manufacturers, and the innovation to extract oil, are great examples of capital.

Social capital is what emerges through the markets and transactions within cities for the common good. Information, trust, and cooperation through churches; social networks like bars, neighborhoods, formal homeowners' associations, and so forth, are examples of social capital. Without property rights most of these examples would not exist. That is why the Founding Fathers placed such an emphasis on property rights.

Even more importantly, limited government was established to prevent the leeching of capital. More on this later.

Because of these fundamentals, America propelled itself into the Industrial Revolution, while (ultimately) leaving the rest of the world behind. Without government intervention, markets were capable of functioning in an efficient manner, providing opportunities to those risk-takers who chose to invest in America's vast natural resources, technological advances, and industry. From colonial times to this day, the United States has experienced a flood of immigrants (both illegal and legal), all trying to enter the United States to benefit from this capital.

All of society, rich or poor, benefits from a free-market economy. These immigrants understood this as well as the Founders, whether they could articulate their understanding or not.

Can this cycle last forever? It certainly lasted for well over two hundred years.

Unfortunately, over time, large stable societies become breeding grounds for numerous special interests (small groups)[1] that threaten to consume the majority's capital through their political and economic agendas. Capital consumption takes precedence, and robs society of the accumulated-capital base needed to sustain a dynamic economy. This is the exact reason why American freedoms have been in jeopardy since the 1890s. Interventionism, progressivism, liberalism, and socialism are simply the same radical agenda swirled together in a toxic stew designed to provide a small, powerful group with the force necessary to enslave the majority.

Unfortunately, during the Great Depression, the economic and political policies that were established by

---

[1]   The United States' population is slightly over 300 million people—a large and diverse group—so when we speak of small groups, that can mean anything from the Federal Reserve to the oil companies, banking institutions, Wall Street, agricultural groups, etc.

the Founding Fathers were replaced with policies that radically changed America's path, and threatened her future. To be sure, many of the "progressive" mechanisms were already in place (for example, the graduated income tax) at the time of the stock-market crash in 1929. But the impetus for central control of Americans gained a new head of steam. The New Deal, Franklin Delano Roosevelt's massive set of proposals for government action, ushered in a decay of freedom that led to economic and political policies that benefit politicians and special interests, instead of the public.

The Great Depression brought overwhelming interventionist ideals that created large bureaucracies. From this point, the formation of numerous small groups resulted; these special interests control the capital of Main Street, USA via their tenured relationship with the politicians in Washington, DC.

Because of these connections, support, subsidies, and special privileges have been given these special interests (this has been going on for over a century). The nation's population, as a whole, is no longer represented by their elected official (and never were represented by the army of political appointees). These individuals have seen the opportunity to advocate policies that benefit them financially.

Therefore, Congress has passed legislation, in the millions of pages, to support these special interests, which in turn guarantee their re-election.

Tragically, roughly 75% of today's economy supports this agenda, either directly or indirectly. The continued payments to these special interests through central control is what has changed America from a capital-accumulating society to a capital-consuming society.

And that's where the danger lies.

* * * *

Capital-accumulation is a fairly basic concept: it's saving, spending less than you earn, and can also be called wealth-accumulation.

Capital consumption is also a fairly straightforward concept: spending more than you make, accumulating debt (like credit-card balances). It's like taking a bunch of your money out of the bank, stacking it up in a pile of twenty-dollar bills as high as you can go, and lighting it on fire.

Capital consumption is best described, as a practical matter, as follows:

- Government and its regulations (the more government there is, the faster capital is consumed)
- Government programs (meaning just about all government activity in the present day, especially so-called "entitlements")
- Taxes
- Automobile industry
- Bailouts (also called "corporate welfare")
- Housing industry
- Interventionism (related to government programs)
- Consumer goods (all types)
- Inflation

Capital accumulation is best described as the following:

- Stocks, Bonds, and Securities
- Real Estate
- Savings (of all kinds)
- Natural Resources (both discovery and exploitation)

Obviously, there is not much point to accumulating capital if it is never consumed. On an individual level, owning a house (real estate) with no furniture (consumer goods) wouldn't be worth it. On a government level, no government at all is as bad as an over-reaching, confiscatory despotism. Similarly, a government administrator paid $90,000 a year who saves the taxpayers a million dollars a year is a good investment; one that exists simply to tut-tut and tell you how badly off you are, not so much.

In short, there must be a balance, but tilted toward capital-accumulation. Long-term capital-accumulation yields benefits for society as a whole.

Capital, by its nature, flows to the parts of the world where the most efficiency occurs in production. At one time, America was such a place. This fact lay behind the innovation, wealth, and the constantly evolving economy that we as Americans once cherished. The American capital-accumulating agenda stood apart from the policies of most of the rest of the world, which remained mired in outdated, ancient practices.

The principles of property rights, minimal government, and low taxes were instilled in our country's leaders and the business community, creating the foundation for a vigorous economy and for a prosperous society. More importantly, these values held that corruption, external meddling (government control), and waste were bad things that should be avoided to the greatest extent possible.

This firm stance against corruption, government control, and waste can be explained by two factors: prior experience (paying attention to history) and cultural traditions rooted in work, opportunity regardless of class, religion, and human rights. These factors reinforced resistance to unethical, illegal, and improper business dealings.

Countries with extremely weak social capital and inappropriate government institutions, on the other hand, cannot effectively benefit from capital, thereby diminishing entrepreneurship and hard work, thus minimizing sustainable economic development. The benefit of enforcing property rights and a capital-accumulating agenda allows future generations to become better off than previous ones. A free society makes mistakes without penalty; those mistakes yield discovery; competition and an invigorating entrepreneurial spirit result.

Most of the world has never been like that. And no country in the history of the world was able to establish those rights like the United States of America.

Where did we go wrong?

* * * *

We believed, during difficult times, in something for nothing. A free lunch. However understandable the cultural shifts (especially religious shifts) over the last hundred years, Americans have traditionally laughed at the concept of a free lunch. Americans knew better.

When someone offered you a free lunch... There was always a catch. And there was never any such thing as "something for nothing."

But we forgot all that in the turbulent 1930s.

There is an old historical force, at least four hundred years old in American history: the force is actually a group of people, and they're called "levelers." And just like *real* market forces, they come and go. That is, their impact grows or lessens in cycles. One of the earliest levelers was Oliver Cromwell. The most recent ones you can see on the news: they're the ones constantly crying about "the one percent." Even though they, themselves, belong to that group (or aspire to it: think about that).

Oliver Cromwell: Early Leveler

In the first half of the 1600s, England fought a civil war that resulted from the one time the English people beheaded their king. For about twenty years, Oliver Cromwell ruled England as a dictator (this was the same period in which the Pilgrim set sail first for Holland, and then for what became Plymouth. Cromwell was noted for, among other things, wanting to make sure that everyone earned the same as everyone else. It was a fool's errand, and shortly after his death, the crown was restored.

Levelers try to make everybody the same. They play group against group. (And yes: you should ask yourself why, because the answer is not that they care about you more than themselves).

And they traffic in lies, and the biggest lie is that they can make everybody the same, and they can undo every perceived injustice in the world by taking wealth from somebody else.

And that is the biggest lie of all.

For it is the market order that exists. "Equality" cannot be achieved. Ever. If it could, the former Soviet Union and present-day Cuba would have been a happy paradise full of happy people, and the world would have been trying to get in (and their citizens would not have been trying to get out).

And yet to this day, people want to believe in that fantasy.

But there are two laws which can neither be repealed, nor can they be ignored. One has to do with physics, and the other is the law of supply and demand. Even in the old Soviet Union, with all its central control and tyranny (the two *do* and must go together), markets emerged, and a barter economy for desired things (like Levi Strauss blue jeans) held sway.

If the government stays out of markets and allows individuals to make choices, we know that markets function efficiently in terms of determining prices for goods and services, based upon mutual agreement between buyer and seller. Prices and consumption ebb and flow, rise and fall, in a natural cycle. "The latest hot thing" which costs an arm and a leg this week will eventually become cheap as producers respond to consumer demand (think about how expensive cell phones were in the 1990s, or even earlier). Likewise, high-cost things like surgery will also decline in real cost.

We know what you're thinking: and no, what we just said is true. Relatively high-risk surgeries, such as vision-correction and cosmetic procedures, have declined in actual cost over the last twenty years because insurance and other third parties stayed out of the market. More on that idea later.

Free markets and competition are good for the consumer.

In a truly free market, anyone can compete. But the opportunity to compete is not a guarantee of success.

Once third-party intervention begins, markets are no longer truly free. To be sure, some external activity is utterly necessary so as to avoid unfair competition. But external activity, or intervention by third parties, is a cost. It reduces the efficiency in the market that capital craves. Examples of external (third-party) intervention include:

- Insurance companies
- Federal regulation
- State regulation
- Federal "assistance" payments
- State "assistance" payments
- Unions

It may seem at first glance that such intervention is a "good deal." It *always* sounds better when you think you can get someone else to pay the costs. But the tongue-in-cheek Golden Rule applies: whoever has the gold, makes the rules. And if some entity outside of your free-market negotiation is making the rules, then you no longer have a free market. And those third parties always come at additional cost—additional cost, that is, to *you*.

Consider this rather exotic example.

Suppose you go into Bueno Taco, a franchise that now operates near where we live. You order their largest burrito, but it comes to you with scarcely any lettuce at all. You now have two choices: complain or never go back. If you go back, you have two newer choices: ask for enough lettuce this time, or do nothing, hoping the previous event was a one-time bad deal. In this example, you and the vendor, Bueno Taco, are the parties to the transaction; the two of you "make the deal" to mutual satisfaction—or you, as the consumer, choose to go elsewhere.

A pure free-market negotiation.

Suppose, however—and this is the "rather exotic" part—someone screams to someone else in Washington, DC, that there "ought to be a law"; that "everyday people are being cheated by insufficient lettuce on tacos." Eventually, the wheels of the bureaucracy would grind into motion, creating the Bureau of Proper Taco, Burrito, and Other Such Food Construction, with federal agents in each and every outlet for each and every vendor of fast-food tacos in the entire country—all posted there to assure that you would get the minimum amount of whatever in your tacos, burritos, and other such foods.

What would happen to the price of your burrito?

You already know: the price would increase. A lot. But what of the time required to make your taco, burrito, or other such food?

You already know: that time would increase also, making your fast food noticeably less fast.

Two kinds of cost added, all because someone thought there "ought to be a law." And you pay both of them.

* * * *

Why, then, do third-party payers thrive?

As the American population grew, and the political culture began to stray from the Founding Father's principles, opportunities to distort those basic principles shifted political rhetoric toward un-achievable ideals. This drift in American politics also created huge vote-getting machines for self-interested politicians. Think about it: it's always easy to promise something for nothing, a free lunch. You'd vote for that, right?

Any small group—a generic term, in this case, for "special interests"—that pressured candidates to support their special privilege at the expense of the nation took precedent over free-market principles that had once benefited the consumer. These small groups could be corrupt building contractors in big cities who pad their bids for public-works projects; huge agricultural interests like sugar growers or dairy farmers, who benefit hugely from archaic crop subsidies; or even certain inside-track defense contractors (should Lockheed Martin really be awarded contracts for cutting the grass at American military installations?).

But this is how things have "evolved" over time, such that support is given by elected (and appointed!) officials to select groups in American society, groups far smaller than the majority, with their interests ahead of the interests of the country as a whole. This is not new, but these small groups began significantly increasing their control (and accompanying monetary benefit) through their political connections since the Great Depression. And since that time, the career-minded politician has reaped the benefits from the small groups that he or she has supported, while the public has not recognized these behind-the-scenes dealings. Hard-working Americans try to raise their families, stay married, and enjoy their precious free time. Keeping an eye on corruption so as to prevent it or root it out—which was once the purview of the press—is a time-consuming task.

Consider the impact of the decision by elected (and un-elected) officials to support special interests over the public at large. What you will see is the beginnings of a corrupt network that does not take responsibility for its actions, regardless of the impact on the country.

Let us examine some of the special interests supported by government officials over time. Some examples include: agriculture, the oil industry, the welfare system, labor unions, banking, the auto industry, insurance conglomerates, and the steel industry. This is by no means a comprehensive list! But all of these examples (and more) have been subsidized, given price supports, protected by tariffs, or given other special incentives. And the clamor for more, more, more continues, as if "the government" actually had money of its own. All the while, the taxpayers pay the cost, or Uncle Sam prints more money when the tax base cannot support the accompanying government bureaucracy.

These special-interest-supporting actions by government officials interfere with the thriving-market phenomenon and threaten to bankrupt America.

A reasonable person might be tempted to ask, yet again: how did this happen?

The New Deal is a big part of the answer. Ideas that sounded good at the time were given the force of law. Indeed, the Great Depression was a trying time for all industrialized countries, the United States and Germany in particular. Old-age insurance (aka "Social Security") was enacted on the German model, and taxpayers had *no choice but to pay* (though the authors are acquainted with a number of people who avoided paying for years, yet collected full benefits).

A briefer answer to how this happened? Third-party (federal) intervention.

During World War II, Franklin Delano Roosevelt enacted wage-and-price controls by executive order (Executive Order 9328). Not by an act of Congress, signed into law, but by an instrument which would have the Founders spinning in their graves. In short, he simply dictated the action. As a result of the dictated wage-and-price controls, companies pressed to find good talent in order to support the war effort by fulfilling their contracts couldn't compete for qualified labor with higher-wage offers. Therefore, the idea of medical insurance as a form of compensation sprang forth.

Third-party (first Presidential, then insurance companies) intervention.

Executive Orders by President

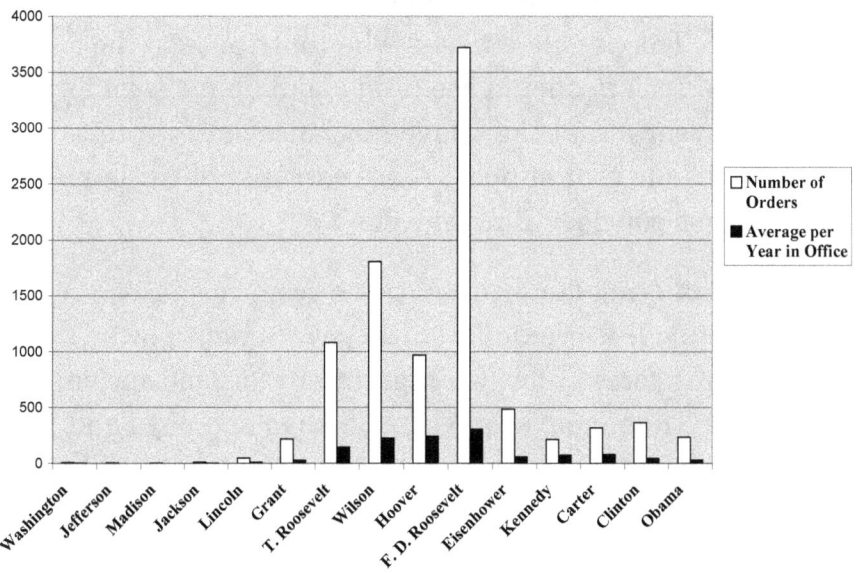

(Source: *The Presidential Project*)

The nuclear age only accelerated third-party intervention. Were it not for the Taft-Hartley Act of 1947, it's likely that all workers would be compelled to join unions in order to hold a job. Instead, Congress awoke to its duties to the public and its liberties, although many states remain "union states" despite diminishing union membership. Nevertheless, union activity in Washington, DC has netted a vast array of specialized regulations far in excess of those needed to ensure a fair workplace.

Third-party (union) intervention.

Third-party payers are the main reason the United States has reached a turning point in its history, both economically and politically. Interventionism has become a corrupt behind-the-scenes movement that applies its forceful agenda to monetarily benefit themselves and the bureaucracy. Tax-paying citizens who contribute to the betterment of society should see (and should have seen for at least fifty years) that they have no choice but to vote out the politicians that support these corrupt political and interventionist policies. But they don't.

And the unifying factor in all these scenarios is federal (and to a lesser extent, state) government power, which gives the force of law (or regulation) to some special interest. And the taxpayer pays. And pays and pays and pays...

There is no risk for special interests involved in these practices when the capital is guaranteed by a government that supports these small groups. This is the exact type of tyranny that inspired immigrants to flee numerous foreign countries and emigrate to the United States. If there were some reasonable limit set for these expenditures, perhaps they could be managed in the hurly-burly that is our political world.

But the increasing size of special-interest groups, along with the increasing *number* of such groups, have forced more and more capital away from production and prosperity, instead to be funneled into the coffers of these small groups. And what is President Barack Obama proposing? Still higher taxes, more spending and debt, simply to support these selfish elites during the most enduring economic hardship this country has faced since the Great Depression. To make matters worse, his would-be successors, Hillary Clinton and Bernie Sanders, either want to continue the old policies, or worse, pile more and more of the same on top of the old wreckage, as if more debt and more taxes will fix what they already ruined.

Tax Cuts are Fun

Everyone likes tax cuts. Taxpayers like them, of course. But Congress and the President like them too, under certain circumstances. In the brief period when the Clinton administration ran a surplus, coincidental with the pending Presidential candidacy of Al Gore, Clinton's Vice President, a tax cut was enacted, and trumpeted throughout the land by a loyal media. And the tax-cut itself?

Repeal of the federal excise tax on telephones (meaning the traditional land-lines).

Most individual telephone subscribers saw savings of less than a dollar a month, but some saw as much as about a buck and a half. You see, this tax was levied in 1898— yes, **1898!**—to pay for the Spanish-American War. Back then, only "the wealthy" had telephones. And like all good taxes with a limited goal, long after the revenue had been received for the intended purpose, the tax kept paying more and more revenue as more and more people got telephones.

Finally someone woke up and decided the "good press" was worth losing the few hundred million a month in revenue. Besides... The country was running a surplus... And so a tax-cut was born, by repealing the tax passed to pay for the Spanish-America War.

More than a hundred years *after* the Spanish-American War ended.

To be sure, the Great Depression invigorated (but hardly originated) this type of corruption in government;

and today we see that same posturing by government (at all levels) to perpetuate support for myriad special-interest groups. Because of this, just like during the Great Depression, the so-called "recovery" has stalled out for the last seven years. And as a result, trillions of dollars have been printed (another form of debt) to try and save the bureaucracy.

So in America today, the majority (the tax-paying public) continues to be unrepresented, manipulated, and forced into accepting higher taxes, a devaluing of the American dollar by the Federal Reserve, and a political-economic agenda supporting none of the Founding Father's principles. "The government" has infiltrated numerous institutions which interfere with free-market dynamics, and that interventionism supports the institutions, the special-interests, and the politicians.

Not the people.

The corporate bail-outs that occurred in 2007-10 are an excellent example of just how powerful these small special-interest groups have become. None of them were held accountable for their part in the financial crisis. The Wall Street crime spree, led by banking and mortgage institutions like Goldman Sachs, Bank of America, Wells Fargo, Merrill Lynch, etc., were the culprits in this latest home-value implosion. Shamefully, these organizations were also the ones that benefited from the bailouts with 0%-interest money from the Federal Reserve.

Here's how it worked: large banks made what were called sub-prime loans to borrowers who would not otherwise qualify for a mortgage because of spotty work history, low income, low credit ratings, or the like. Those loans went out at approximately 4%, depending on when the loan was made. The money used to finance those mortgages came from the Federal Reserve at 0%, and that was all taxpayer money, either in the form of actual funds, or freshly printed money, which (through inflation), reduced the value of the dollars you had in your pocket. And then, when the sub-prime buyers defaulted, the big banks went, hat in hand, to Uncle Sam to get their guaranteed loans repaid—with another dose of taxpayer money, whether borrowed or printed. And to cap off the Big Lie, the President told you on TV that these institutions were "too big to fail."

"Too big to fail?" "Too big to survive" is more like it... If "too big to fail" were true, dinosaurs would still roam the Earth.

And then, of course, everyday people who might have squeaked by found their homes dropping in value, and if things came to pass that they couldn't sell their houses because they were worth less than what they owed... They defaulted, or held out until the bank foreclosed on them, whether the bank was a big bank or a small local bank. That drove prices down further, dragging more people into the financial sewer.

Federal money flowed from the political leaders that supported the special-interest groups, which led to these politicians being re-elected. It is a disastrous circle of corruption that supports the political machine, rids society of prosperity, and propels the capital-consuming agenda.

This cozy arrangement must cease for the good of our country.

The lobbying effort in America has become more powerful than the representation of the people. The elected politicians (and their un-elected regulation-issuing counterparts) in DC have the special interests in mind when executing public policy, not the interests of Main Street, USA. These small organizations realize that over time, capital will remain under their control only so long as the politicians supporting their small group stay in office. And all the while, the assistant-to-the-politician stands waiting in line as the next interventionist to take over the reins, after his predecessor retires from political service with hordes of taxpayer money.

A good example of this is Chris Dodd, the former Democratic senator from Connecticut. Dodd recently retired after his career in politics and is now a lobbyist for the Hollywood elites. Dodd, a liberal Democrat (perhaps we should drop the pretense and call him a socialist), should have been scrutinized for his role in the collapse of the housing market. Dodd, along with Barney Frank, Bill Clinton, Al Gore, Alan Greenspan, Robert Rubin, Franklin Raines, Andrew Cuomo, Larry Summers, et. al., essentially re-invented the Carter-era Community Reinvestment Act (1977). They just renamed it the Affordable Housing Act, and increased its scope. Their vision was, once again, to provide home mortgages to Americans with terrible credit ratings and the likely inability to pay their government-guaranteed mortgages. These were termed sub-prime loans (even the name should terrify you).

What ensued from this interventionism was the financial crisis of 2007-2008, which will be examined in greater detail later. For now, let's examine interventionism (third-party intervention) in more detail.

Government

When government intervenes to support institutions in an economy (for example: automobile manufacturers, banks, telephone companies, energy companies, etc.), the free market loses its efficiency in what economists call "discovering" interest rates, prices, wages, and profits. (In other words, the free market is distorted and unable to work properly; supplies and demand are subverted to fit the needs of special interests.) This distortion feeds on itself, causing irregularities in other markets, leading to additional government intervention so as to sustain the original (government's) intent. Of course, more intervention to fix a previous intervention should seem foolish at best and criminal at worst.

Doesn't seem to work out that way...

In this scenario, government is not protecting the market economy; instead, it is careening toward socialism in its effort to "improve" (interfere with) the market. Because of this invasion, the consumer's choices do not affect the marketplace, and an unrealistic economy emerges—benefiting special interests, not the consumer. Experience demonstrates that tax-paying consumers are the ones who get to foot the bill called inflation.

Always.

A good example of this is how the Federal Reserve ("the Fed") has intervened in the marketplace when it comes to interest rates. Since the 2008 bailouts, the Fed has taken whatever measures it likes in order to keep interest rates artificially low. As a result, the consumer has experienced an increase in the cost of food, fuel, insurance, rents, and so on (in other words, inflation, no matter what the "official" pronouncements claim). And all because the Fed has decided to devalue the American dollar by printing money, so as to maintain a 0% borrowing cost, all to support the failed banking institutions in America.

This action has caused massive deficits (translated: your children and grandchildren get to pay for them), closing in on $20 trillion.

That's $20,000,000,000,000,000.

Has the consumer benefited from these lower interest rates? Has the unemployment rate fallen since this policy was enacted? Of course not. Instead, Americans are forced to experience even more intervention, and still have not seen a rebound in economic activity for some time.

The official unemployment rate no longer has any accuracy; its calculation has long since been subverted, to the point that no mathematician could support it. Personal incomes have not risen to keep up with the rate of inflation. Apparently none of these corrupt policy-makers have read their history books; intervention has been attempted in the past in large societies, and it has never worked.

In fact, such policies turned out to be the exact cause of those countries economic turmoil, and ultimate total collapse. The Soviet Union and even ancient Rome are great examples.

A large portion of Americans, perhaps most Americans, and particularly young Americans, cannot properly define "socialism."

Socialism is government ownership of the means of production—everything. Being a "democratic socialist" changes nothing: socialism, in any flavor, is still government ownership, not private ownership, of business.

Similarly, the bailouts of failing institutions such as AIG, General Motors, Bank of America, Goldman Sachs, etc., creates partial government-ownership of those institutions, creating a mixed economy that does not support free-market principles. The welfare class in America has been bought off by a socialistic agenda for decades, and the upper class is enjoying an unchanging, corrupt relationship with Washington, while the middle class has felt the most pain.

And the middle class is shrinking...

Financial collapse and the eradication of the middle class faces the United States and Western Europe today. The collapse of the economic and financial systems is a consequence of the interventionist policies Western governments have introduced in their societies. Debt takes over that society, because the tax burden placed upon the productive middle-class can no longer support the government's profligate spending. The following chart displays the tax rates in Western Europe, proving that interventionism leads to higher taxes in order to support socialism. (The VAT, or "value-added tax," is the national sales tax that is forced upon European citizens.)

Bear in mind: this doesn't include any other forms of tax, such as property taxes nor automobile taxes (called "registration" in the United States, but it's a tax). Nor so-called "sin taxes," nor gasoline taxes...

United Kingdom

Income Tax: 50% VAT: 17.5%   TOTAL: 67.5%

France

Income Tax: 40% VAT: 19.6%   TOTAL: 59.6%

Greece

Income Tax: 40% VAT: 25%   TOTAL: 65%

Spain

Income Tax: 45% VAT: 16%   TOTAL: 61%

Portugal

Income Tax: 42% VAT: 20%   TOTAL: 62%

Sweden

Income Tax: 55% VAT: 25%   TOTAL: 80%

Norway

Income Tax: VAT: 25%   TOTAL: 79.3%
54.3%

Netherlands

Income Tax: 52% VAT: 19%   TOTAL: 71%

Denmark

Income Tax: 58% VAT: 25%   TOTAL: 83%

Finland

Income Tax: 53% VAT: 22%   TOTAL: 75%

Unions

Let us make ourselves clear from the outset: unions were a good thing in the nineteenth century. Why and how unions came into being makes perfect sense. During the Industrial Revolution, when there were utterly no precedents to draw from, finding ways to provide safe working conditions, decent wages, and to provide for laborer's old age had to be found (economists call these things "selective incentives"). But after achieving these things, the unions' power grew like cancer over the decades, such that the original selective incentives became irrelevant.

A famous example from American history tells much.

The Pullman strike in Pullman, Illinois began on May 11, 1894. This cataclysmic event marked a turning point, the time when politicians realized the importance of siding with unions to gain the votes necessary for election (or re-election). This tragic episode was regarded as the most violent nationwide strike up to that time, and exposed the power of nineteenth-century corporations as they used violence against labor-union protests.

The Pullman Palace Car Company employed nearly 4000 union workers at its plant on the west side of Chicago. Due to an economic downturn in the economy in 1893, often called the Panic of 1893, the lack of demand for these rail-cars had diminished. This situation forced the owner of the company, George Pullman, to lower wages and reduce production (or else go out of business entirely). At the same time, the cost of living for

Pullman's workers did not go down. Most importantly, rents on company-owned housing in which the laborers resided remained unchanged, and this circumstance prompted a backlash from the workers.

> The Panic of 1893 was caused to a large degree by railroad overbuilding and questionable financing of that building. (Sound familiar?) Until the Great Depression in the 1930s, it was considered the worst event of its kind in American history. The irony with respect to the Pullman strike is, of course, that the Pullman strike itself took place not only within the railroad industry, but the railroads were ultimately used by the striking union members to wage "strike warfare."

The Pullman workers were not, as yet, members of the American Railway Union (ARU), which had over 250,000 members nationwide (this changed during the strike when Eugene V. Debs, the president of the ARU, conducted a rapid recruitment of Pullman workers). This led to a call by Debs for a total nation-wide boycott by the ARU—from switch-men on the lines to the porters loading and unloading the Pullman train cars, to the yard-workers who attached and detached Pullman cars. The strike inevitably forced the Pullman Company to shut down its factories.

George Pullman, an entrepreneur, had no choice but to hire non-union workers to replace the striking union workers, and provide protection for those non-union workers that crossed the picket line. The ramifications led to violence between business interests and the unions, eventually affecting economic prosperity across the

United States (in short, making the Panic of '93 worse). Property was destroyed and violence increased.

Tension between the two sides escalated into a riot in which thirteen railroad workers were killed and more than sixty wounded. President Grover Cleveland declared a violation of the Sherman Antitrust Act by the union workers, claiming that the strike threatened public safety. Moreover, the strike halted the delivery of the United States mail, a critical consideration at the time. Cleveland mobilized the Army to restore order, along with the United States Marshals Service, with orders to break up the strike. The strike-organizers and the President of the ARU, Eugene V. Debs, were arrested and jailed for causing the uprising. It appeared the event and, more importantly, its effects, had come to an end.

Debs studied the works of Karl Marx during the time he spent in prison. He was subsequently released in 1895, and became a leader in the socialist movement in America, running for President of the United States five times as the Socialist Party candidate.

Later in 1894, after the strike had been settled, in an attempt to pacify his stormy relationship with organized labor, President Grover Cleveland pushed Congress to pass legislation to create Labor Day as a federal holiday. The Supreme Court later reviewed the Pullman case and found that the employer, The Pullman Company, not just the union, had also caused the strife. This reversed the original Supreme Court decision, which had been taken in the heat of the moment.

But still more effects resulted from the strike.

John P. Altgeld held the Illinois Governor's chair during the strike; he was also the head of the Illinois delegation to the Democratic Party. Altgeld despised the support offered to The Pullman Company by Cleveland. Altgeld wielded his power and used his relationship with the unions to generate enough votes to block Cleveland's re-nomination at the 1896 Democratic National Convention, which was held in Chicago. Altgeld succeeded in his efforts, which demonstrated the potential power of the relationship between politicians and labor unions. This cozy relationship continues in our political system today.

In 1898, the Illinois Supreme Court dissolved The Pullman Company and divested ownership to the town, which was then annexed into Chicago. From that point, politicians realized how important it was for them to support organized labor in order to benefit their (re-)election. In the Pullman case, the employer lost his right to make a voluntary choice regarding labor, thereby losing his economic freedom and, ultimately, control of his company through the force of government.

From the Pullman Strike emerged the relationship between politicians and union members—only one of the century-old capital-consuming policies that continue to control American tax dollars. What we have today is a President, Barack Obama, who sides with labor unions (and consequently regulating businesses further into a decline), and not for the benefit of the country, but for political reasons only.

We must ask ourselves: did Barack Obama, a product

of the Chicago political machine, study this logic or is it simply the Democratic torch that continues to be passed along by the insiders originating with the Pullman strike? The same principle applies today in America. All the free-riders continue to control larger and larger shares of capital—corruption that Karl Marx ignored in his much-vaunted, and equally much-flawed, theory of labor. Marx clearly created the political rhetoric underlying unionization. In America, the motivation of labor unions is no longer the benefit of their members; instead, it is for more and more money for more and more political power, and the control over wages and pensions.

But it's not just trains. Older readers will recall the name of Jimmy Hoffa, the teamster-union boss, whose criminal activity was so egregious that even his Democratic friends were compelled to abandon him, and see him go to jail for racketeering.

And, naturally, his son was elected head of the Teamsters some years later.

But more recently, a case in Wisconsin exposed the ugly, corrupt relationship between teacher's unions and the public treasury.

Wisconsin Governor Scott Walker recently proposed legislation to do away with collective bargaining for the teachers' union in that state, which uncovered the corrupt union agenda supported by the Democratic politicians in that state. A heavy majority of the school districts in that state faced a deficit of $500,000 or more because the teacher's insurance company was owned and operated by ... the Union! To no one's surprise, the rates being charged to the teachers were the highest in the nation.

One of the more interesting facets of the Wisconsin teachers-union brouhaha was the attempt by the Democratic legislatures to illegally shut down the legislature by not showing up (and thereby thwart the reforms described in this chapter). Under the Wisconsin legislature's rules, it was mathematically possible to shut the house down if the Democrats disappeared. So they did exactly that, hiding out in motels and other places while paid demonstrators rioted for the benefit of network news. Nevertheless, the AWOL legislators were found and compelled through legal means to perform their legal duty. To your authors' knowledge, none of these miscreant "legislators" were charged, despite their conduct being highly illegal.

The Left clearly adheres to the old Leninist dictum: the end justifies the means. When they can't get what they want through the legislature, they're clearly willing to break laws, even if doing so contradicts the will of the taxpayers.

Every year the cost for that union-owned insurance rose, promising to bankrupt the state, further causing higher and higher taxes to pay for the fraud. What transpired from this immoral, unethical activity was the union insurance company funneling millions to re-elect the Democrats that supported the existing situation (over-priced insurance packages for teachers being only part of the problem).

What a great racket!

Taking tongue out of cheek, it was a great racket for

the tiny group of insiders; for the public, and for the teachers themselves, it was a raw deal, to say the least.

Shining the light on this dishonesty has apparently exposed such corruption in other states. Collective-bargaining agreements are presently under fire in Ohio, Indiana, and other near-bankrupt Midwestern states. Because of Governor Walker's tenacity, along with the steadfast devotion of the legislators who wrote the new reform laws, union corruption has been exposed, and the Wisconsin Teachers Union now offers a much lower insurance rate.

The bidding for insurance was put out to the private sector—an open competition, in other words, for the first time in decades—and consequently, some of the Wisconsin teachers district unions are now enjoying a surplus, and the taxpayer is not on the hook for supporting the corrupt network. Has any of this been broadcast across America by the media? You know the answer to that.

Don't you wonder *why not*?

Clearly, the liberal left will not admit to any unethical practices on the part of their powerful union allies. Union power must be pruned, and drastically, back to a level that's good for their members and good for the country. Despite their shrinking membership, they continue bankrupting states and municipalities because of similar corrupt and unethical practices. Keep up the good work, Governor Walker, and the people of Wisconsin.

Labor unions today are experiencing a decline in

membership, but continue to receive an enormous amount of taxpayer money through the political agenda of President Obama. The ratio of taxpayer money to union members is preposterous. Union membership is now smaller than ever, yet the organizations remain just as powerful, and control the largest amount of capital in Big Labor history.

Three

Consequences

It's one thing to point to corruption. While the consequences of such unethical (and sometimes criminal) behavior might seem self-evident, things don't always work that way. And you might not even think you care. But you do, or you should. Consider the following cases.

Tragically the current economic crisis in America was caused by a dismantling of the Founders' vision of prosperity yielded by limited government. Instead, through the interference and force of institutions, government officials control our monetary and fiscal policy. It has become evident that, over time, the comfortable relationship between unions and our political parties has caused more and more corruption. This intimate arrangement has allowed capital to flow between the two small groups (i.e., government officials and unions) benefiting from their association with one another.

This corruption is never taken into account by the neo-classical economic models used by these "experts." In those models, human behavior is not considered at all, and only the behavior of prices with respect to supply and demand, and how quickly those two factors change relative to one another, are calculated.

Yes: no consideration of human behavior...

For that matter, calculations of human behavior never

turn up in the worthless supply-and-demand illustrations taught at our universities. Before the Great Depression, corruption on the part of government officials in America was simply not tolerated (for example, the Tammany Hall affair in the nineteenth century). And in the twenty-first century, corruption is simply ignored, as if it didn't exist.

Tammany Hall: Corrupt Government in Nineteenth-Century America

Tammany Hall's roots lie in the eighteenth century, when the political organization was founded. Its infamy lies, however, in the nineteenth century, when William M. "Boss" Tweed ran the organization, and with it, New York City. His political career also included a term in the House of Representatives and the New York Senate.

"Boss" Tweed's utterly corrupt machine was also utterly efficient. Tweed traded influence for votes by delivering favors to various groups within New York, and silenced opponents with bribes. That the things he did were illegal seemed to mean nothing: even after the Tweed ring was broken up, one writer wondered in print, "why it took so long to throw the rascals out." And had it not been for a crusading journalist (whatever happened to those people?), Thomas Nast, the Tweed ring might have continued. (Tweed tried to bribe Nast; Tweed failed.)

Tweed stole (according to original estimates) between $25,000,000 and $45,000,000 of taxpayer dollars—which was much, much more in the 1870s than it is in 2016. Later estimates of the amount he stole neared $200,000,000.

Even now, accounting for such thievery is difficult, so you can imagine how difficult it was in the 1870s.

You have to ask yourself: do we have the same situation now as New York had a century-and-a-half ago? And if we do, why is no one doing anything about it?

"THAT'S WHAT'S THE MATTER."

Boss Tweed. "As long as I count the Votes, what are you going to do about it? say?"

Government was not seen as the financial savior of the needy prior to the Great Depression. Churches and charitable groups provided that salvation; the government was simply *not involved*. Because of this non-interference, improvement in economic conditions throughout the United States resulted in a higher standard of living found nowhere else in the world. These invigorating economic policies were accepted throughout all aspects of political and economic debate, and the welfare of the nation was the utmost concern. This was the primary objective in economic and political policy during the eighteenth, and the majority of the nineteenth, centuries.

After the Great Depression, politicians claimed to have no choice but to create government programs to support the needy. In theory, at least to many, these were temporary measures (but consider the Spanish-America War tax example above). Regardless, no bloated, engorged bureaucracy was envisioned like the one that fiscally enslaves us today.

As the population grew, and political vision strayed further and further from the Founding Father's principles, distorted promises of a "better life" (not to mention a "free lunch") replaced the Founders' vision with one that shifted political power to an increasingly corrupt, paternalistic political machine. Special interests gained momentum and power through this relationship, supporting their capital-consuming agendas.

Subsidies, price-supports, and other special incentives and privileges resulted from this change in the political environment around the time of the Great Depression. And since then, the career-minded politician has reaped the benefit from whichever small groups he or she supports, while taxpayers have largely not noticed these behind-the-scenes dealings. When government officials decide to support special interests in lieu of the tax-paying public, nothing can come about but a corrupt network, which takes no responsibility for its actions.

Grandma used to get upset when she saw someone engaging in what she called "robbing Peter to pay Paul." To her, such behavior was immoral, and ought to have been illegal (if it wasn't already illegal, of course). Even more to the point, she always viewed robbing Peter to pay Paul as ineffective. And yet that's what's happening today, 24/7/365. In more formal terms:

> It is when we come to the proposed measures of relief for the evils which have caught public attention that we reach the real subject which deserves our attention. As soon as A observes something which seems to him to be wrong, from which X is suffering, A talks it over with B, and A and B then propose to get a law passed to remedy the evil and help X. Their law always proposes to determine what C shall do for X or, in the better case, what A, B, and C shall do for X. As for A and B, who get a law to make themselves do for X what they are willing to do for him, we have nothing to say except that they might better have done it without any law, but what I want to do is to look up C. I want to show you what manner of man he is. I call him the Forgotten Man. Perhaps the appellation is not strictly correct. He is the man who never is thought of. He is the victim of the reformer, social

speculator, and philanthropist, and I hope to show you before I get through that he deserves your notice both for his character and for the many burdens which are laid upon him. [...]

Such is the Forgotten Man. He works, he votes, generally he prays—but he always pays—yes, above all, he pays. He does not want an office; his name never gets into the newspaper except when he gets married or dies. He keeps production going on. He contributes to the strength of parties. He is flattered before election. He is strongly patriotic. He is wanted, whenever, in his little circle, there is work to be done[...]

Professor William Graham Sumner wrote those words.

In *1883!*

What we have been describing are only the latest in a long-running series of manipulations. The current miscreants didn't come up with anything new; nor have they come up with any truly original ideas.

People will take from others when conditions are right; such corruption *must* involve the people in power. This is evidenced in recent years by the unstable American economy. Consider the following examples of corruption and unethical politics, which continue to consume our capital and have put a stranglehold on the middle class.

Four

The Federal Reserve

The foundation of the interventionist pyramid and, ironically, the smallest (yet most powerful) group is the Federal Reserve. The Fed, as we have come to know it, was established under the Federal Reserve Act of 1913, with the power and mission to dictate stable monetary policy. Establishing this entity (a revived Bank of the United States) was one of newly elected President Woodrow Wilson's priorities.

The original act established a minimum of eight but no more than twelve districts throughout the United States. It was formed as a reaction to numerous financial panics in the early 1900s and earlier. The purpose of the Fed has evolved over time, from the initial responsibility of maintaining an elastic currency to today's duties of conducting monetary policy, supporting a stable United States dollar, and providing financial services to banking institutions, the federal government, and foreign banks.

Of course, if a group has the power to dictate stable monetary policy, by definition that group also has the power to dictate *unstable* monetary policy...

The appointed individuals who serve on the Federal Open Market committee (FOMC) has seven members, and the twelve member Federal Reserve bank presidents are comprised of both public and private banking, individuals offering a so-called balanced approach for the decisions made that affect American interest rates. It has also been referred to as the "Bank of Banks," or the "Central Bank."

The Gang of Twelve?

The Federal Open Market Committee (FOMC) consists of twelve members—the seven members of the Board of Governors of the Federal Reserve System; the president of the Federal Reserve Bank of New York; and four of the remaining eleven Reserve Bank presidents, who serve one-year terms on a rotating basis. The rotating seats are filled from the following four groups of Banks, one Bank president from each group: Boston, Philadelphia, and Richmond; Cleveland and Chicago; Atlanta, St. Louis, and Dallas; and Minneapolis, Kansas City, and San Francisco. Non-voting Reserve Bank presidents attend the meetings of the Committee, participate in the discussions, and contribute to the Committee's assessment of the economy and policy options.

The FOMC holds eight regularly scheduled meetings per year. At these meetings, the Committee reviews economic and financial conditions, determines the appropriate stance of monetary policy, and assesses the risks to its long-run goals of price stability and sustainable economic growth.

The FOMC, the twelve district bank presidents, and the Federal Reserve chairmen, are independent of the United States government. *By law, they do not have to seek authority from the President or the Congress of the United States to institute policy.*

The analysis of economic statistics, banking regulations, and the overall status of the economy is what influences the Federal Reserve's monetary policy on interest rates. Ever since the gold standard was dropped by the Nixon administration in 1970, the Federal Reserve has kept interest rates artificially low, as a general statement. Meanwhile, housing markets saw an incredible leap in prices; therefore, home-equity increased, while incomes barely kept up with the rate of inflation.

Over time, the Federal Reserve has deserted the taxpayer, and abandoned its mission. For instance, under Alan Greenspan, who was appointed as Federal Reserve Chairman in 1987, the Federal Reserve decided to change the equation that determined the Consumer Price Index (CPI). The CPI measures the inflation rate (the change in prices of what everyday people buy, but not such things as securities, real estate, or taxes) for the American consumer on a monthly basis. The CPI is sometimes referred to as the *cost of living index*. This economic statistic is widely watched to determine the movement of interest rates by the Fed.

Prior to 1987, food and energy costs constituted a larger percentage of the CPI, which reflected a higher inflation rate, thereby requiring the Federal Reserve to keep interest rates higher to ward off the threat of inflation to the economy. One might wonder why Greenspan and his colleagues decided to change the CPI equation. *We* don't.

Greenspan's method, sometimes referred to as "let them eat hamburger," assumes that the consumer will make choices for the lower-cost goods and services. For example, if the price of steak is too high, then the consumer will purchase hamburger. So the "let them eat hamburger" argument puts a larger percentage of the CPI calculation on goods and services that are cheaper and a smaller percentage of the calculation for expensive goods and services.

This new CPI calculation reflected a lower standard of living, and lower payouts for Social Security and federal salaries, since the cost-of-living adjustments for those payments are determined by the CPI. Greenspan's new calculation saved the government money, and hurt American retirees that had paid into the program. Most critics of this change do not agree with the calculation of the CPI, because it reflects a lower inflation rate, not to mention distorting long-term comparisons to previous decades.

The inflation rate would reflect a 7-10% increase per year if the United States used the original equation. Obviously, the American consumer requires food and energy to survive, and can acknowledge that the true inflation rate is much higher than the bogus figure that the government prefers to report. If the inflation rate was as low as is being reported these days, the consumer would be enjoying an expanding, vibrant economy not a dead, shrinking one. But due to Alan Greenspan and his successors, along with the other members of the Federal Reserve, we see American interest rates that have been kept artificially low. The end result of this type of monetary policy has created asset bubbles, which lead to boom-and-bust cycles, which prohibit genuine economic growth.

Truthfully, we all know that the rate of inflation is higher than reported by the government. The pain being felt by the consumer because of declining home values has prevented credit-expansion through home-equity lines-of-credit to continue the false economic boom. At the same time, the size of the special interests have not decreased, causing more capital to be funneled into these small groups by the government officials. And what does President Obama (and his two hopeful successors, Hillary Clinton and Bernie Sanders) propose? Still higher taxes and still more federal spending to support ever more special interests, all during the most enduring economic hardship this country has faced since the Great Depression.

The scandalous relationship between the Federal Reserve and the investment banks like Goldman Sachs also raises questions about the history of the Federal Reserve. When founded, the Fed was chartered to support the banking system, then to support the dollar, with a view to achieving full employment. Today, the Federal Reserve has in a sense become a world-wide savior, a non-transparent printer of money. And worst of all, they support whomever and whatever they choose, as Americans witnessed in the bailouts of 2008. Where did all the money go?

Consider a few examples...

The investment bank, Goldman Sachs, has continued to reap the benefit of its insider relationship with government for decades, due to its senior executives being appointed by past Presidents to serve as Treasury

Secretaries (as well as the so-called "czars" in the current Obama administration—and czars are the *last* thing Americans need). This fact is critical to understanding the factors underlying the housing crisis, and the subsequent bailouts that were initiated by our government and the Federal Reserve. Countless unanswered questions persist about the particulars of that bailout. Why can't we get answers?

Yet taxpayers are constantly tapped for more taxes for still more bailouts and subsidies, and their wealth is stolen daily by hidden inflation. The interventionist insiders are behind this, and the tax-paying middle class is fleeced without knowing it.

Has anyone been prosecuted for this destruction of the middle class? Short answer: this particular elite, Goldman Sachs, has retained incredible power over the bureaucracy in America. When such power becomes this entrenched, capitalism no longer contributes to national prosperity. Instead, the monetary benefit goes to the corrupt.

A Czar By Any Other Name is Still a Dictator

After 2008, Americans saw a parade of "czars." An energy czar, a this czar, a that czar... In short, someone appointed by the President to have sole authority over whatever emergency had been declared that particular week.

The czars ran Russia before the 1917 revolutions (some would argue that the Communist Party that replaced them were just other czars). The point is that czar and kaiser have the same origin: "Caesar." And Caesar killed the Roman republic, and, more importantly, was a tyrant.

Why do you want a government that thinks solving problems requires appointing a czar—a Caesar, a tyrant, a dictator with no oversight by anyone?

Consider one of the most important unanswered two-part questions. Why did Goldman Sachs receive 100% of its investment in AIG during the bailout? In addition, why was Goldman Sachs permitted to become a bank within twenty-four hours of the announcement of said bailout?

Evidently it was because the Treasury Secretary under President George W. Bush, Henry Paulson, was a former Goldman Sachs executive. It goes further than that: Bill Clinton's Treasury Secretary, Robert Rubin, was also an ex-Goldman Sachs executive, who held office for ten years. Ironically, Timothy Geithner was Robert Rubin's assistant secretary during his Clinton-era reign. And the buddy-system continues: numerous representatives in the Obama Administration are old

Goldman Sachs executives. How many? There are at least *twenty* retired Goldman Sachs employees currently in the Obama administration.

How convenient is that? Wasn't this institution the leading firm that sold mortgage-backed securities to other investors, and contributed to the housing crisis and the financial collapse of the American economy? The same firm that then sold the insurance on those securities, knowing full well that the insurance policy on those mortgage-backed securities was a fraud? And then Goldman Sachs received metaphorical trainloads of interest-free (that's 0%) taxpayer money (debt) during the 2008 bailout. This allowed them to continue enjoying million-dollar bonuses for their executives at year's end, and to continue the same old corrupt practices.

Granted, the CEO of Goldman Sachs, Lloyd Blankfein, had no choice but to lie when called in front of Congress to discuss the firm's corrupt role in the financial collapse. Big surprise. But more importantly ... with absolutely no repercussions whatsoever.

Now the good old boys are manipulating the stock market, controlling its advances and declines with all of the printed money while the other 99% of Americans are losing their homes, jobs and belief in the American Dream.

Goldman Sachs isn't the only such banking firm, but they are perhaps the most blessed. Or the most connected.

The long-time investment-banking firm, Lehman

Brothers (founded in 1850) declared bankruptcy in 2008 after a mass exodus of clients, plummeting stock prices, and a host of other financial pressures. Nevertheless, a bailout was not in the cards for this company.

We find it appalling that two weeks before the Lehman collapse, which was the first domino to fall, Ben Bernanke and Henry Paulson stated that the "banking system in America is sound and functioning." Two weeks later, the disaster commenced as the rest of the dominoes fell.

How soon we forget the facts from the beginning of this bust. We have asked over and over, ever since that statement: why should we believe *anything* that Ben Bernanke or *any* government official has to say about such matters? How can anyone claim these self-proclaimed economy-managing wizards have any credibility whatsoever when they couldn't see the collapse coming?

Unless, of course, they were lying...

Then, to add insult to injury, Americans were assured that elephantine bailouts were the only way to save the economy because, these self-anointed financial wizards claimed, failure was not an option. Bernanke and Paulson proposed the first bailout, which amounted to just under one trillion dollars.

Yes. $1,000,000,000,000.

The interventionists bailed out the interventionists. They promised the American people that this influx of taxpayer money, which was simply more debt for you and your descendants in disguise, was the "stimulus" needed to avoid a total world-wide financial-system meltdown.

And here we are, eight years later, and the Federal Reserve has not turned off the printing presses, churning out digital worth-less dollars by the billions, and will not reveal where the money is going ... all while President Obama (with Congress' complicity) has spent ten trillion dollars under his fiscal policy efforts. That's ten trillion dollars *more than the US Treasury took in*, that is...

It's hard to wrap your head around a number like 10,000,000,000,000. But consider this measurement. If you started counting when you were five years old, and *never did anything else*, you couldn't get to 10,000,000,000,000 before you died.

Ben Bernanke was appointed Fed chairman by George W. Bush after Alan Greenspan retired in February, 2006. Before that, Bernanke was a Federal Reserve Governor (2002-2006), and prior to that held the economics-department chair at Princeton University. He claims that he studied the Great Depression inside and out, which gave him the expertise to control the recent economic collapse of America.

The notion that any individual has the knowledge, wisdom, and skill to control the mechanisms of a modern, diverse economy is ludicrous. Such false claims yield the ultimate absurdity: watching the financial markets wait for the latest big announcement by these corrupt individuals plotting the course of America economic activity.

Bernanke has continued to tout the aforementioned static neo-classical model, which takes no account of an over-leveraged government or consumer credit—or human behavior and frailty. (At the end of 2015, consumer debt in America exceeded 23.4 trillion dollars—that's $23,400,000,000,000—due to the irresponsible manipulation of interest rates by this corrupt elite, offering more credit than most individuals could pay off in their lifetimes. That total has, without doubt, increased since then, and Sanders, according to some, wants to add another thirty or so trillion so we can "spend our way to prosperity.")

The Federal Reserve, countless Obama administration officials, connected economists, and corrupt investment-bankers have claimed the recession was over since 2010, nattering on and on about "the recovery." Such statements are easy to make from a well-connected ivory tower, when you are connected inside the small group that *benefits* from churning out money. In the meantime, a major segment of our society remains helpless as mortgages are foreclosed and houses lost, jobs disappear, with no hope in sight for a remedy. None of those trillions of dollars have benefited the middle class. We can only hope that the truth gets out and taxpayers will take action.

And where are we? Friends, these interventionists have piled up more than $18,000,000,000,000 in debt (please note: it will be a lot more when you read this!) between the Bush II and Obama administrations, all while lying to and manipulating the American people. These charlatans *can't fix anything!* It would seem that lying is about the only skill these incredibly powerful figures have mastered—and while the free-lunch magic-show goes on, our economy, and the middle class' prosperity, have hit a brick wall.

You might be asking yourself: why do I care? Maybe you're "doing OK" in your estimation. Stay with us, because you care more than you know.

Thomas Jefferson said it best:

> I believe that banking institutions are more dangerous to our liberties than standing armies. If the American people ever allow private banks to control the issue of their currency, first by inflation, then by deflation, the banks and corporations that will grow up around them, will deprive the people of all prosperity—until their children wake up homeless on the continent their fathers conquered.

Thomas Jefferson gave this warning to Americans over two centuries ago.

Five

The Rogue's Gallery

Before going into detail as to why you care about all this (presuming you don't already care, that is), let's look at the players in this drama.

President Obama could have ended the fraud and double-dealing we have described, consistent with his preaching about the need for change during his 2008 Presidential campaign. Instead he chose to surround himself with the interventionists; Rahm Emanuel, Larry Summers, Jon Corzine, Harold Raines and Timothy Geithner. These individuals were groomed by the old interventionists, allowing for the cover-up and fraud to continue.

So much for "hope." So much for "change." So much for "transparency in government."

Consider Jon Corzine's career at Goldman Sachs and in politics. Corzine was the Goldman Sachs CEO in the late 1990s, and was replaced by Henry Paulson in 1999. Corzine subsequently began his career in politics. Corzine, a Democrat, was elected as a Senator from New Jersey in 2000. He refused to produce tax-returns during the campaign, which would have revealed the 400 million he made after taking Goldman Sachs public in 1998 (which also nearly bankrupted Goldman Sachs). He served five of his six-year term as Senator, choosing to enter the New Jersey governor's race in 2006.

He won.

In the 2010 New Jersey election, Corzine lost to Republican Chris Christie. After ten years of "public service," he was recruited by MF Global, with salary and bonuses exceeding $725,000,000 for less than two years of employment.

Such a trail should leave you scratching your head at minimum.

Corzine joined MF Global, and within a year of his start-date, MF Global sought bankruptcy protection, losing over $1,000,000,000 (that's *billion*) in customer wealth. Apparently nobody, not even Corzine himself, can explain where the money is.

The bankruptcy occurred because of an all-in bet on Western European bonds, which are now worthless. No doubt because of his connections to Goldman Sachs and the Federal Reserve, MF Global became a primary dealer to the Federal Reserve in February 2011.

Within eight months of becoming a primary dealer, MF Global sought Chapter 11 bankruptcy protection.

One must ask: did the Federal Reserve and Ben Bernanke examine MF Global's balance sheet properly when deciding primary-dealership status? Or did the connections Jon Corzine gained throughout his private and political life influence the Federal Reserve's decision?

It's entirely possible that the Federal Reserve may have simply overlooked (or ignored) MF Global's all-in bet on Western European bonds. As far as we're concerned, the Federal Reserve and its members demonstrate daily an uneducated approach to solving the American financial crisis. In fact, they have contributed to it.

But Corzine is hardly the only rogue in the gallery.

Starting in 1966, Robert Rubin began a twenty-six-year career at Goldman Sachs, where he and Corzine sat on the management committee in 1980. Rubin later became a Goldman Sachs co-chair, and a senior partner in 1992 (his final year with the firm). President Clinton chose Rubin as his Treasury Secretary; Rubin held office all eight years.

Larry Summers and Timothy Geithner both served (if that's the right word) as Assistant Treasury Secretaries under Rubin during the Clinton administration. Rubin, along with Alan Greenspan and Larry Summers, led the charge to get the Commodity Futures Modernization Act passed in 2000, keeping over-the-counter derivatives-trading from being monitored by the Commodity Futures Trading Commission (CFTC). (The CFTC had in 1997 denied the requests by Greenspan and Rubin to keep such trading out of CFTC oversight.) Rubin managed to get this changed, with Greenspan's lobbying assistance, all under the guise of "modernization."

Modernization Isn't Always Improvement

An over-the-counter derivative is millions of dollars of mortgages bundled into a single mortgage-backed security. This security can be traded like stocks and bonds. As long as housing increased in value, there was no problem. Unfortunately, sub-prime mortgages were included in these bundles, but their ratings were set at AAA, instead of the much lower ratings they deserved. Without CFTC oversight, brokers and big banks could lie to investors.

Why did the Clinton administration want this deregulation? Was their social-engineering agenda so important that they wanted to shatter the middle class? This question is especially important, since the insiders could sell these securities short, which is just another form of insider trading. And insider trading is a felony.

Removing oversight of the over-the-counter derivatives market is what enabled Goldman Sachs and AIG to sell the house-of-cards loans we have described earlier in this book. And it was those (effectively) unsecured loans that yielded the collapse of America's financial system.

Why have we labeled these individuals as rogues?

In 1995, Greenspan (with assistance from Rubin and Summers), pressed for legislation to deregulate the trading of mortgage-backed securities and derivatives. This was in keeping with then-President Bill Clinton's desire to have another try at home-ownership for the poor (the mortgages required to do this are called sub-prime loans). As a result, the Affordable Housing Act was implemented in 1996, which loosened credit and earning requirements for home ownership.

This created a problem: since no banks wanted to take the risk, Greenspan pressed to deregulate (with Clinton's oversight, one must conclude) and the two men intervened in the market (and abused their power). The Commodity Futures Modernization Act was passed, which deregulated the mortgage-backed securities and derivatives, which allowed Wall Street to pass on the risk of these sub-prime loans to the taxpayers. The loans were guaranteed through Fannie Mae and Freddie Mac (two hybrid organizations that are, in effect, government-owned companies, backed by taxpayer dollars).

Brooksley Born, head of the Commodity Futures Trading Commission at the time, refused to implement the risky deregulation. Pressure from Clinton, Greenspan, & Co. compelled Born to resign on June 1, 1999. Clinton signed the Commodity Futures Modernization Act into law on December 21, 2000.

While the terminology is the same as Reagan-era marketplace reforms, what we're describing here is exactly the opposite: not a reform at all, but a situation in which people were unleashed to speculate in land. Land speculation (and speculation in general) has been at the heart of a number of financial disasters in American history:

- The Panic of 1837 (land)

- The Panic of 1897 (railroads)

- The Great Depression (stocks purchased on unsecured margin)

- The so-called Tech Bubble around the turn of the twenty-first century (tech stocks)

- The so-called Great Recession beginning in 2008 (land again, not unlike the unsecured purchase of stocks in the 1920s prior to the Great Depression)

Seven years of corrupt, unethical trading ensued, creating great wealth for the Wall Street banks, supported by Greenspan and his cohorts. Who benefited? The corrupt elite benefited, the insiders who foisted their intervention on the marketplace even though it wasn't in your interests at all. And as a result, taxpayers that were supposedly being championed lost their homes, jobs, and, in some cases, their retirement savings.

Not Only Are Not All Banks Created Equal, But Not All Banks Do the Same Sort of Financial Work

In this book, we discuss the actions of investment banks and retail banks—primarily investment banks. It's important for us to point out that these don't do the same sort of work. An investment bank handles stocks, bonds, and other securities, as well as securities that are related to mortgages. But not necessarily mortgages themselves. A retail bank, however, is the sort of street-corner or mall-located store-front bank where you have your checking and savings accounts. Maybe you got a mortgage there; maybe you didn't, but you could.

Rubin and Summers pressed for legislation to overturn the Glass -Steagall act of 1933, which prohibited investment-banking institutions from engaging in the retail side of banking. Because of the repeal of Glass-Steagall, investment banks could then create the mortgage-backed securities and sell them on the open market, which also contributed to the financial crisis in 2008.

You have to wonder: if it was a good idea to prohibit such banking practices at the height of the Great Depression, why was it a good idea to repeal that law?

After Rubin wrought all this damage, he left public service and was offered a position with Citigroup in November 2007. Shortly thereafter, he was given the chairmanship. Rubin resigned as chairman in November 2009, with an easy take of more than $125 million in compensation for his tenure at Citigroup.

Now, let's be clear: we have nothing against CEOs being paid large salaries. But $125,000,000 for two years? Even we have to say that's far too much, especially given the foul trail of corruption he blazed to get there. We doubt he had his stockholder's interests at heart during that period, either.

Larry Summers succeeded Rubin as Treasury Secretary in 1999 and stayed in the job until 2001. Before that, Summers had been the Chief Economist for the World Bank from 1991-1993. He won't be remembered for his economic studies, or his Presidency at Harvard; instead, he'll be remembered for his lack of oversight and understanding of the mortgage-backed securities market. Despite this, Summers is back teaching at Harvard, enjoying a large salary and benefits. But he has *not* been held accountable for his defrauding of the American people.

Henry Paulson, insider-trading expert and former Goldman Sachs CEO, has enjoyed similar remunerative benefit from his role in the financial crisis. Paulson joined Goldman Sachs in 1974, working for the firm in Chicago; he became a partner in 1982. From 1999-2006, he held Goldman Sachs' chairmanship. During that time, he accumulated millions, and then left for public service (again, if that is the right term).

George W. Bush appointed Paulson Treasury Secretary, which position he enjoyed from 2006-2009. Now the trail leads back home. Both Paulson and Bernanke assured the American people that their banking system was solid. Two weeks later, the two had the pleasure of explaining the total collapse of that very same financial system.

But!

They also assured Americans that a bailout of $800 billion was the only option to save the system. Why did Congress believe them?

That $800,000,000,000—and $3,500,000,000,000 more—has been handed out to the institutions and individuals responsible for this domestic disaster, and *not one person has been held accountable!* The people who caused the problem escaped with hundreds of millions, and continue their capital-consuming reign over the American people. Paulson and Bernanke had the pleasure of picking and choosing which firms would fail, and which firms would be merged with other firms, and which firms would collect billions in bailout funds.

And let's not forget: everything we describe in this book required an act of Congress when we discuss legislation. How did your Representatives and Senators vote?

And none of this insider-dealing did a damned thing for Main Street, USA. The only beneficiaries were the chosen institutions and the "public servants" supporting those institutions.

When will the whistle-blowers come out of the closet? Juan Williams comes close, but still defends President Obama's (and the Democratic interventionists') policies. One hopes that Bob Beckel's rhetoric is scripted when he offers his views on the Fox News. Beckel's assertions that archaic "entitlements"—all deeply rooted in the corruption plaguing Washington, DC—are effective and helpful to the country are patently absurd. His vision of Barack Obama as a great President and the answer to America's problems is worse than that.

Six

Understanding Monetary Policy

Americans today generally think that "monetary policy" is a recent thing. Far from it. The ongoing argument predates the Constitution.

After Yorktown (1781) came the Treaty of Paris (1783), which brought peace between the erstwhile colonies (now the United States of America) and Great Britain (things moved a lot slower then). Instantly the question arose: who would pay the individual colonies' war debts? And ... with what?

Rest assured: the argument was long, heated, and at times, even vitriolic.

You can't have a country without two things: an army and a treasury. Everything after that is window-dressing. American monetary policy became not only a real thing, but a real problem, starting in 1783.

Alexander Hamilton and Thomas Jefferson wanted to solve the problem. They were also political enemies, even though they were both fierce supporters of an American Constitution. At the risk of over-simplification for the sake of space... One wanted a solid, rock-steady currency based on gold (enough gold in the treasury to exchange on demand for any dollar bill in circulation); the other wanted however many un-backed paper dollars it would take to pay the debt.

At least they both wanted to pay the debt...

The debate between greenback dollars (probably the only kind you have ever seen, though they also used to come in red and blue) and gold-based currency began, and raged in varying degrees throughout the nineteenth century. Usually the greenback people came from frontier or farm country (debased currency helped them "pay" their debts more easily, so they could own their land outright) and the solid-currency people came from big cities, with ties to financial interests. (Would you loan money if you were only going to get half of it back? Of course not.)

For a time, some people would no more take a greenback dollar than they would a wooden nickel.

A little over a hundred years ago as of this writing, William Jennings Bryan was setting the agricultural Midwest afire figuratively with his "Cross of Gold" speech. In brief, the gifted orator refused to "be crucified on this Cross of Gold!" The metaphorical reference was as obvious as it was effective. He wanted silver-backed currency, and he mobilized his constituents, who wanted the same thing, with heady, emotional appeals to their deepest-held spiritual beliefs.

At least Bryan and his fellow-travelers wanted dollars backed by *silver*...

During World War II, the FBI and the larger Treasury Department worked tirelessly in a counter-espionage effort to prevent the Germans from printing bogus dollars and British pounds. The German effort was, of course, aimed at undermining the Allied war effort by debasing their currencies.

A few years ago, many Americans first heard the term, "quantitative easing." Fancy term. And if the speaker is feeling lazy that day, or merely has a penchant for acronyms, they just say "QE."

Funny how accustomed we have become to bureaucratic acronyms in lieu of real words. Newspeak if ever we heard it.

Quantitative easing is printing money. Just like the Germans did in World War II. Except now we have banks of computers dispensing digital dollars instead of greenbacks. So much cheaper and quicker that way...

But *you* are the one who pays.

The monetary-policy war isn't over. We'd be surprised if ever it was.

* * * *

Given the chance, historians will tell you, over and over: governments that print money devalue that currency as a result, causing prices to rise (inflation). Examples they would give you abound. It's important to remember that, in the twenty-first century, this doesn't mean actually printing more dollar bills, as it did in previous centuries. In fact, the federal government ruthlessly pursued counterfeiters for decades (and still do). During World War II, battalions of FBI and Treasury agents pursued mercilessly Nazi counterfeiters who sought to destabilize the dollar (and the British pound) as a way to damage the Allied war effort.

So when we say "printing money," again, we mean the issuance of dollars that Uncle Sam doesn't have, via electronic transfer.

The Federal Reserve over the last several years has printed trillions of dollars, kept interest rates artificially low, and attempted to support an overvalued stock market. These actions are all short-term fixes and will not support long-term growth. They support inflation and corruption. And yet the Federal Reserve continues to report a stable, non-inflationary economy.

Taxpayers should be outraged. Why aren't they?

The debasing of a currency by printing more money has only resulted in disaster in the past. The individual creditors who financed the American Revolution were ruined by the worthless colonial script that was used to re-pay them for their wartime loans (the lack of a single unified currency was one of the reasons for the formation of the United States from the thirteen colonies). The French Revolution was partially caused by egregiously excessive spending, which included French financial and military aid to the colonies.

We already told you the story behind "QE" (liberals are good at changing the names of things when the things they foist upon us are proved faulty—hence their re-adoption of the name "progressive"). We know that America has lost its credibility throughout the world because of these manipulative money policies, along with massive over-spending by the Bush II and Obama administrations.

In fact, America's credit rating was lowered not long ago, for the first time in history [and of course the President appeared immediately on television to tell us that 1) he disagreed profoundly; 2) that the lowering of the American credit-rating was groundless; and 3) everyone knew the truth—though one must wonder about the actual meaning of the third item on this list].

How does QE affect us? Investors world-wide have decided not to participate in the quarterly auctions that are required to refinance the spiraling debt in America (meaning, in other words, that private investors no longer want to "buy our paper," meaning they don't think the United States is a good risk any more). So what resulted from that? The Federal Reserve decided to print still more money, buying up toxic debt from the investment-banks, and the investment-banks have the understanding from the Federal Reserve to participate in the quarterly auctions. In our estimation, this activity is no different from a Ponzi scheme.

In fact, investment banks are currently receiving money at 0% interest from the Federal Reserve, and then the Fed is paying them 4-5% interest for participating in the auction and holding the debt. Spot the Dog could make money in this no-risk arrangement (as long as Spot was an insider, of course).

When such policies are enacted, the economy experiences an increase in the cost of food, utilities, fuel, and everything else consumers need and want. At the same time, incomes stagnate and unemployment surges. The exact economic decline that the United States and Europe are experiencing today demonstrates this. The long-debunked methods forced upon American taxpayers by "our" government is doing nothing for the working class, and nothing for Main Street, USA.

The second decade of lost growth and prosperity looms.

Putting it simply: flooding an economy with money impoverishes people and ruins their lives. The consequences of this money-printing agenda by the Fed doesn't include prosperity. The so-called recovery helps no one but well-connected insiders.

The boom-and-bust cycles over the last thirty-five years, caused by the monetary policies instituted by the Federal Reserve, have not yielded a steady stream of growth—no matter how things may seem. Consider the examples of housing and cars, the two largest-ticket items that American consumers buy.

The irregularities in the Fed's monetary manipulation, which created the perception of an economic boom, meant the (imaginary) boom could not be sustained. Americans have witnessed that sad reality for the last eight years. Because of low interest rates, the housing market experienced a false increase in home values, and offered consumers false equity against which to borrow, in order to purchase capital-consuming goods (many of which are manufactured outside of the United States, which exacerbates the unemployment problem).

The so-called boom (1998-2007) was completely based on credit. Granted, unemployment was low, but once housing lost its excessively-inflated value, the house of cards fell in. Consumers had become accustomed to using previously unheard-of equity in their homes to take out easy-to-get lines of credit, purchase automobiles, flat-screen televisions, etc. Suddenly they found themselves trapped in the middle. Yet policy-makers refused to prevent this ridiculously unsustainable housing bubble. Why?

Because the elites that caused this false prosperity were becoming filthy rich off those unwitting consumers who participated in this fake economy...

One must ask: why didn't we learn from Jimmy Carter's Community Reinvestment Act of 1977, which led to the 1987 savings-and-loan disaster? (You might have noticed: savings-and-loan institutions are gone, destroyed by the malfeasance). Older readers will also recall the double-digit annual inflation during the Carter years. Younger readers might want to ask oldsters they know how that worked out for them (hint: it wasn't good).

The point is this: the insane monetary policy we have described is exactly what was used in the past, except now it's being referred to as "quantitative easing." (See above for what happens to the names of things when the public figures out the falsehoods and untruths.) The Federal Reserve hasn't changed a thing. The Fed money-mill has printed trillions of dollars, just since 2007. Consequently, the value of the dollar has declined by more than 30% over the last decade. Meanwhile, the Fed continues its false claims: "there is no inflation"; "the economy is recovering"; etc., etc., etc....

Every consumer who's paying attention—male or female, young or old—knows full well this is a lie. If you doubt us, just pick a product at random at the grocery store—maybe that family-sized jar of peanut butter. It has easily risen 40% in price, if not more, in the last ten years of "no inflation."

Fairy tales are fun, but not when the fairy tale is the one about the healthy twenty-first-century American economy.

But the problem runs deeper than this, and goes back even before the Carter years.

In 1971, President Richard Nixon canceled the convertibility of dollars to gold (since the founding of the Republic, any holder of dollars could convert them to gold bullion on demand). Despite the promise that this was only a "temporary measure," like virtually all government "temporary measures," it became permanent in 1973, when the dollar was allowed to "float."[1] This meant the value of the dollar was determined by the Federal Reserve's monetary policy.

Since that time, the dollar has no longer been set to "the gold standard." Instead, the Federal Reserve was given the responsibility of supporting and preserving the dollar. So-called "stagflation" in the 1970s because the

---

[1] The dollar, until 1971, was fixed at the price of gold: $35 per ounce. This rate was constant and underlay the long-term reliability of the American economy.

Federal Reserve began printing more dollars than needed. Inflation rose as those "worth less" dollars rolled off the printing press by the billions.

In spite of this nearly half-century-old decision, the American dollar has been the worldwide currency (since it replaced the British pound after World War II, largely because of similar political decisions taken in Britain in the 1940s, making the veritable pound less reliable). The dollar, held to the gold standard, fluctuated against other countries' currencies (more appropriately, we should say that those currencies floated against the dollar). The American government nevertheless guaranteed that any dollar would be backed up by a set value, in gold. In response, for example, European countries and Japan purposely devalued their currencies in order to stimulate their exports and increase economic activity in the aftermath of the Second World War.

It is high time that the American public realizes the damage being done by this powerful entity. Until the Fed is dismantled and new blood is brought into government at all levels (new blood that represents the taxpayers instead of the establishment), the most powerful small group in America will continue to manipulate the United States and her economy. Otherwise, the Fed will continue devaluing the dollar, and thereby stealing more and more of *your* hard-earned wealth, by perpetuating a bankrupt monetary policy that has *never* worked.

It Doesn't Have to be This Way

American political life slowly, over decades, changed from representing all Americans to representing a corrupt clique of insiders, pushing high-minded (and horribly flawed) ideals in public policy, all of which benefited one group and one group *only*: themselves. Congress has made the decision to support special interests and the small groups consuming Main Street's capital. Now, America's arteries are clogged with corruption because of these policies, the taxpayer has been forgotten, and there seems no end in sight.

But it doesn't have to be that way...

When the ruling class reaches the type of dominance it has in the United States today, when the ruling class abandons all sense of honor and accountability to the governed, when the ruling class serves only themselves, the only solution is to cleanse the system of these corrupt individuals and institutions.

War has been the instrument for such cleansing in years past, but we hardly believe Americans want that. But we still have the Constitution, and we still have the vote. And we have examples of what can be. Chile's experience shows how genuine reforms can turn around a corrupt society.

The Miracle of Chile shows how a corrupt communistic society, controlled by corrupt small groups, can become a vibrant democratic society. This evolution occurred from 1970 to 2000, and has continued to benefit the robust economy that Chile enjoys today.

In the early 1970s, Chile's inflation rate was off the charts, with limited trade and a Gross Domestic Product utterly at odds with the vast wealth in natural resources found in the country (for example, copper and other minerals and seafood). The popularly elected government was overthrown and replaced by a dictatorship—in other words, people were elected by promising the voters something for nothing, a free lunch at the expense of somebody else (sound familiar?). Ultimately, powerful forces within the country ousted that government and set the country on a new path.

Let's make one thing clear from the outset: we don't want armed insurrection or a coup to happen here. What we *do* want is for readers to draw the useful lessons from Chile's example, so that such violence won't happen here.

Augusto Pinochet led the military coup in 1973. His vision for his country evolved from his realization that the oppression of the masses by a government that controlled all aspects of Chile's economy did not benefit everyday Chileans. The Chilean central bank was printing money by the bushel to pay off the skyrocketing debt compiled in previous years, a large portion of which expenditures had simply lined the pockets of the corrupt rulers and their minions. Pinochet and his followers decided that the crooks had to go.

Make no mistake. It was a bloody coup, but in the end it benefited the entire country. After the coup, Pinochet summoned a group of economists known as the Chicago Boys, alumni from the University of Chicago who had studied under Milton Friedman. They recommended free-market reforms that instituted appropriate deregulation and privatization. This strategy allowed those same free markets to create economic prosperity. These policy changes took time, but what transpired for the Chilean people is a country that has privatized its pension system, state industries, banks, and reduced its taxes. All of these measures have allowed Chile to become a vibrant economy ranked third in the Americas with a Gross Domestic Product growth rate from 3.2%-5%.

Back to the USA.

America's interventionists have instituted high-sounding policies and programs which have shifted the country from prosperity to corruption. Those who desire a robust, thriving American economy must elect candidates that understand the Constitution, human behavior, and the competitive spirit in not only the 2016 elections, but in all elections, always. Remember, the government does not have rights; only individuals have rights. Corrupt countries experience no prosperity; countries whose governments respect the rights of its people do. Western Europe and America are in the same situation, and it will require strong electoral action—so as to avoid drastic measures such as those used in Chile—to overcome the powerful anti-growth policies instilled by these small groups.

We'll put it to you a different way: the first part of the Chile Story has already happened here. Do you want to see the second part of the Chile Story happen here? Or would you prefer to use ballots instead?

Follow the Yellow Brick Road...

An Illuminating Tale

You don't have to be a Boomer, or even the parent of a Boomer, to know that lyric. While I haven't checked, it's probably safe to say that Judy Garland and her friends are still off somewhere in Netflix Land, or Cable Land, or DVD-Blu-Ray Land, or wherever. Off singing happily as they skip down the Yellow Brick Road.

To the Land of Oz...

My mother saw this movie as a teen-aged girl, when it was new. And in 1939, the technology was awesome: a wide-screen presentation, in full color, no less. *Along with Gone with the Wind*, another wide-screen full-color film, *The Wizard of Oz* ushered in a golden age for Hollywood. (It probably didn't hurt that *Oz* came out mere days before World War II erupted in Europe in 1939, and *Wind* in January of the following year, when things European were horribly unsettled; they gave audiences something else to think about, which is what movies are for.)

My mother loved those movies, and we watched *Oz* any time it was on television during my childhood. In black-and-white, of course, and cropped to a 4:3 screen...

A few years ago, I had occasion to talk to her about the movie, in a completely different context. I think I ruined her life. You see, she thought it was just a silly, happy, fairy-tale story.

The Wizard of Oz is political commentary. *Unvarnished* political commentary! Populist ranting from

95

the Midwest about monetary policy. The *last* thing it is, is a fairy-tale.

Think about it. The symbolism is in the reader's face (*Oz* was a book before it was a movie).

The yellow bricks are gold. Meaning gold ingots, the basis for American money in 1907, when the book was written. Oz, of course, is the abbreviation for "ounce." And Oz, the place, was ... green, the Emerald City being the prime example—in other words, a symbol for greenback dollars.

People in the Midwest wanted cheap, inflated, worthless [*sic*] currency ("greenback dollars") that was *not* based on gold, let alone dollars fixed at $35 per ounce of gold. The book (and the movie, in a manner of speaking) was about the long-running (and still-running) war in the United States over monetary policy.

And the characters? Aside from Dorothy, all the characters were symbols of high government officials and other luminaries of the day.

Yes, it's true: I probably ruined my mother's life...
[MC]

* * * *

All humor aside, the result of the pressure for money not based on gold was added currency based on silver. The ratio (set shortly after the Constitution went into effect) was 15:1. So in addition to a "gold standard," there was also, for most of two centuries, an American "silver standard" as well. But at least those dollars were based on something, instead of the nothing-behind-them greenback dollars like we have now.

In short, monetary policy has been part of American history since before the Constitution was written, and has slipped even into popular culture.

Just watch *The Wizard of Oz*...

No Inflation? Are You Kidding?

The federal government has been telling us for years that inflation is "under control," indeed that there is virtually no inflation at all (this is their excuse to print more money, which causes inflation). They're so adamant about this lie that Social Security recipients didn't get a cost-of-living raise last year. The fact that in this case, "the government" means (particularly) people like Alan Greenspan should worry you, since it was he who changed the way inflation was calculated, making all previous comparisons meaningless without lots and lots of extra math.

Between 1900 and 1975, the dollar shrank to about a third of its value. In other words, what required a dollar to buy in 1900 required three dollars to buy in 1975. Then Americans experienced the Carter years, in which double-digit inflation was the norm—but at least it hovered around ten to twelve per cent. By the middle 1980s, the dollar had dropped to about a fourth of its 1900 value, meaning what required a dollar to buy in 1900 required four dollars to buy in 1985.

Then things settled out pretty well and in fact had settled out by early 1983. Things ran pretty smoothly, inflation-wise, even through the 1990s (the tech boom didn't hurt in that regard, either). By then, of course, the calculation method for the Consumer Price Index had been altered as described elsewhere in this book. And for the last eight years, the pure lie that "there is no inflation" has been pushed down our throats.

We'll bet you know better.

Here are a few measuring points from a hundred years ago. In 1916:

- A loaf of bread cost about $.07—yes, seven cents!

- The average car cost about $400.

- A postage stamp cost $.02—yes, two cents.

- Coffee? Fifteen cents per pound ($.15).

- Sugar? Four cents per pound ($.04).

- The average price for an American house was $5000.

To put things in context:

- The loaves of bread aren't the same (we'll bet the 1916 loaves were better).

- The cars certainly weren't the same (but we'll bet the car-savvy shoppers among you have noticed higher and higher prices over the last seven to ten years).

- Postage? In the 1970s, the United States Postal Service, even with the assistance of trains, airplanes, and truck delivery on interstate freeways, couldn't deliver a letter as fast as the Pony Express.

- Coffee is now a luxury beverage for some, and we didn't mean that kind: we meant the kind you buy in the grocery store, and we'll bet you can't get it for under a buck a pound anywhere (the local Wal-Mart sells one of the old-school brands, Folger's, for $4.16 per pound).

- Sugar's price is inflated [*sic*] beyond what would otherwise be the case by federal subsidies, but even then, it's a lot more than $.24-$.30 per pound (the local Wal-Mart sells it for between $.55 and $.60 per pound).

- We'll stipulate that the houses today are different than the houses in 1916, and the effect of approximately three times as many people living in the United States has an effect, too; but realize that the "average" 1916 price includes the huge mansions on such places as Long Island and other high-priced American neighborhoods.

Some more comparisons:

- Remember half-gallon boxes of ice cream? Try to find one. First they shrank from 16 ounces (a half-gallon) to fourteen ounces about seven years ago; now they're 12 ounces. (Oddly, boxes of ice cream seem to be sold by weight, yet have historically been advertised in fluid ounces.)

- A bar of soap ten years ago was a thick rectangular slab weighing at least 4.75 ounces. Now they're a curved thing with no corners, weighing 3.75 ounces, and they cost more now than they did ten years back.

- Did you ever buy the small trial-sized bottles of shampoo (also real good for traveling)? Eight years ago they cost fifty cents and contained two full ounces. Now they cost a dollar and contain only 1.75 ounces.

- The huge jar of peanut butter (store brand) that could be had for between five and six dollars five years ago now costs over nine dollars.

- Subway five-dollar-foot-long promotions disappeared about three years ago. Now they're six-dollar foot-long promotions: and that's a 20% increase.

- Restaurant chains such as Red Robin, Chili's, and Applebee's, have been instituting radio-frequency paying stations (and some of these restaurants expect you to use the devices to order your meal, too). This allows the restaurant to hire fewer waiters, and reduces the human-interaction at the restaurants to the same level one expects at McDonald's or Wendy's (except in those latter two examples, employees still take your order in all cases). Fans of *The Big Bang Theory* can only wonder what will become of Penny's waitressing job at The Cheesecake Factory.

- Levi's 501s for $20 a pair? Only if you found them on sale or at an outlet store. In 1990. They're more likely to be more than twice that price now.

- Last, and certainly not least: medical insurance costs more than a few years ago, but at the same time co-pays at the doctor's office went up, too. How much you pay for various procedures has gone up. And the amount insurance companies pay for even generic prescriptions has declined significantly (making the cost of medicine to you go up). The amount insurance companies pay for name-brand prescriptions has, in many cases, plummeted dramatically.

In most of the cases above, the inflation is far, far greater than the amount the dollar has "officially" shrunk in the last century (or, in the shorter-term cases, the last quarter-century). The government officials who tell you there is no inflation are either liars or blind fools. Which do you think it is?

Seven

It Isn't Just Monetary Policy...

When government officials believe they should make choices for taxpayers, that society and that economy are no longer functioning efficiently (not to mention the abject immorality inherent in the situation). As we have already demonstrated, politicians and bureaucrats are determining interest rates, who receives the bailouts, and which sectors of the body politic will retain a monetary relationship with the government.

But that's just one facet of the problem.

It is self-evident that "progressives" would rather shun the majority for the sake of their corrupt relationship with organized labor, big oil, banking institutions, insurance companies, and the auto industry—regardless of the pain inflicted on us, the taxpayers.

But hemorrhaging money isn't limited to making elites wealthy. It's also used to maintain the voting base. As we discussed earlier, Americans have been lulled into thinking that there really is a free lunch, and they really *can* get "something for nothing."

What is broadly called "welfare" came into being during the Great Depression, all as part of the New Deal. It had much to recommend it: war widows (from World War I) and orphans needed help because of the economic disaster. Social pressures demanded that men provide, and when they couldn't do that, some of them reacted by hitting the road or even killing themselves. ("Hobos" were a part of popular-culture depiction for decades after the Wall Street crash of 1929, and the images of bankers and other financial "wizards" leaping from the Empire State Building burned themselves into the public's consciousness.) Emerging mass media, meaning radio at this time, joined yellow-journalism papers to drive home the message.

Yellow Journalism: Forerunner of Today's Media Environment

Perhaps the most famous example of so-called yellow journalism is the front-page headline fairly screaming "REMEMBER THE MAINE!" The *USS Maine* was the United States battleship that sank in Havana harbor in 1898. Chain newspapers, in this case the papers owned by William Randolph Hearst, screamed for revenge. The assertion was that Cuban saboteurs, under orders from their Spanish colonial masters, had sabotaged the ship while she lay defenseless in the Cuban harbor. Later investigation—including forensic examination decades later—revealed that no such thing had happened. But by then the Spanish-American War had been fought and Cuba changed hands.

The term fell into use after that, referring to the style of journalism: aggressive, belligerent in fact, unbalanced, and especially inflammatory. But the nickname derived from the cheap paper used to print these newspapers: the quality of the paper was so low and the acid content so high, that they rapidly turned color, becoming yellow far faster than the paper used in books.

Criminals became fashionable. Violent, ugly men like Al Capone, John Dillinger, Baby Face Nelson, and Pretty Boy Floyd became, to some segments of the population, popular figures. To some, they seemed like the embodiment of a bastardized version of the Robin Hood story (Robin didn't fight to take from the rich and give to the poor: he, an Anglo-Saxon, fought Normans to regain control of his lands stolen from him during his absence.) Women like Bonnie Parker (of Bonnie-and-Clyde fame) and Ma Barker even got in on the act. That there is nothing good in what these people did meant little to the confused hero-worshipers of the age.

As the sign at the top of the photo indicates, unemployed men during the Great Depression could receive free coffee and doughnuts. The sharp-dressed man in the white fedora on the far left is Al Capone, the notorious Chicago gangster. Clearly, Capone marketed himself as a sort of Robin Hood in Chicago, even as he murdered his gangland competitors while smuggling illegal alcohol and drugs, ran prostitutes, and so on.

But the fact remained that the economy lay in shambles. To be sure, unemployment never got worse than approximately 25%, meaning that three-quarters of the work-force was still working. But if you were one of the quarter of the work-force that wasn't working, desperate times not only loomed: they were there.

Before the New Deal, responsibility for caring for the needy fell to local churches and charities. Such assistance was short-term because local folks were helping local folks, and one didn't want to be "on the dole" any longer than needed in front of one's neighbors—especially when those same neighbors were paying your bills. In plain terms, people were reluctant to accept handouts.

The New Deal changed this. Interestingly enough, FDR's people pushed for work for payment, whereas the opposition wanted plain payments. The idea was that self-respect could be salvaged if work was performed for the government check. The opposing view held that people would be so ashamed of "being on the dole" that they would get off it as soon as they could.

Obviously, both views had good arguments behind them. But one of your authors wonders to this day how much self-respect his grandfather maintained, sitting by the side of a road, counting cars, when no one did anything with the data he collected. The car-counting grandfather in question pressed hard until he got back with the railroad; we'll leave you to decide the answer for yourself.

For years, drawing welfare payments was called "being on the dole." It was only later that it was called "being on welfare."

Over the ensuing eight decades, however, the original purpose has mutated into a political issue—and a powerful one at that—and it has become apparent that most recipients would prefer never to return to the workforce, instead continuing to receive "free money." It might not be this bad, had FDR's programs been the end of the story. But Lyndon Johnson's "Great Society" increased federal measures by quantum leaps.

The taxpayer's burden has gone up and up and up, while the "War on Poverty" has been a disastrous failure. And while the tax burden has increased, such spending has outstripped the added intake. And as a result, more and more money gets borrowed—either from taxpayers themselves in the form of U.S. Savings Bonds or other similar instruments, or out-and-out borrowing from overseas countries, most famously the Chinese and the Saudis. Yet the welfare system continues to grow as new "social programs" (welfare programs) emerge, initiated by politicians seeking votes for election (or re-election).

The welfare system has mutated from a short-term benefit for those in need during tough economic times, into a capital-consuming addiction, a bureaucratic drag on the economy. Consider these few examples.

- Food stamps (originated right after World War II when it was discovered that too many draftees couldn't serve because of malnutrition—think about Uncle Sam's underlying motivation in that one for a moment)

- Aid to Dependent Children (started during the New Deal to help abandoned or widowed wives and their children, which is now rigged to pay unwed mothers to have more children.

- Section 8 Housing (abundantly flawed, failed Great Society program—if you doubt us, go have a look at "the projects," and see what the trillions of tax dollars have bought)

And of course, we now have a new, shiny example of federal largess: the so-called "entitlement" to free (or subsidized) medical care. That said, "welfare" became a dirty word not later than the 1990s. So the "progressives" (back when they were still called "liberals") renamed it. Now welfare programs are called "entitlements." More on this lie later.

Long-term participants abound. Some are in the fourth or even fifth generation, having learned how to manipulate the welfare system, and having forgotten the self-governing citizen's obligation to contribute to the nation, instilling family values, and providing for one's own existence.

Receiving welfare was frowned upon by Americans in the 1930s. Even men who joined the military as a solution to their economic troubles were looked down upon by large segments of society. Churches and charities helped the truly needy; government was simply not involved at all.

The drill sergeant yelled at a fellow trainee, "Getcherhandsoutcherpockets!" All one word. The trainee had forgotten the lesson all military people learn early: keep your hands out of your pockets. I wondered why, at the time. Years later, the pieces fell into place.

Slackers walk around (or used to, at any rate) with their hands stuffed into their trouser pockets, trying to look cool, probably—particularly in the twentieth century. Since men who joined the Army and other services during the Great Depression were looked down upon (as slackers who couldn't make a living any other way) by many of their fellow citizens, it only made sense for the services to break their new members of this civilian habit—for the good of the individuals and for the good of the services' public images.

Decades later, you can still hear drill sergeants shouting that sentence stuffed into a single word...
[MC]

Until the New Deal. The political genius in its name should be plain as day.

Ultimately, the Depression ended. Most said for years that the Depression ended because of the New Deal (either a misjudgment due to ignorance or an out-and-out lie). That claim is patently false: the New Deal lengthened and exacerbated the Great Depression. But consider this political reality: if you have a whole generation of voters who believe a falsehood, and those voters believe that more of any good thing is even better, what else could you expect?

That's right: more intervention in free markets, more

tinkering by "wizards" and "technocrats" and especially "the best and the brightest."

And personal liberty and your God-given right to pursue happiness, your God-given right to make the most of your abilities, be damned...

For a brief time, common sense held sway. The post-World War II generation, along with the World War II generation itself, voted in enough responsible representatives to put the brakes on runaway liberal programs. Not to end any of them, of course, but at least to slow them down.

In 1996, Bill Clinton, compelled by a Congressional majority backed by its constituents, publicly stated, "Mend it; don't end it." Consider those words: clearly he thought ending some of his precious vote-getting welfare programs actually could happen. Compromise resulted.

The Personal Responsibility and Work Opportunity Act placed control of numerous welfare programs in the hands of the states. Federal funds are given to each state (think about that Nixon-era lunacy: why not just let the states run their programs and never send the money to Washington *in the first place?*). The states then administer the programs. This method met with controversy, push-back from the participants, community organizers, and the Democratic Party in general. Nonetheless, this *bona fide* reform diminished the welfare roles and put people back to work.

Revenue Sharing: the Worst Deal in Recent American History?

It sounded like such a good idea: federal dollars to the states to enhance their various programs. At the time (1970), Uncle Sam had plenty of money (if you think that spending more money than you have means you have "plenty of money"). This was due in part to Nixon's winding down American involvement in Vietnam; moreover, the Johnson-era "tax surcharge" of 10% had an effect on revenue also (not to mention alienating Middle America from the war even further).

So the grand plan sprang forth: Nixon asked Congress to "share" federal revenue with the states. Two *huge* problems:

- Just as electricity is consumed sending electricity from the generating plant to the consumer, so is money consumed moving money from one party to another.

- Taking money from taxpayers, sending it to Washington, and then back to the states gave greater central control to Washington: if any state dared to defy this or that new federal power-grab, DC threatened to withhold funds for this or that project (highway funds being a particular favorite). In any other situation, that would be called extortion. And yes, extortion is a felony.

Of course, the concept grew and grew, just like cancer. And net revenues for 1970 were negative. In other words, the deficits resumed immediately after a one-year budget surplus, which had been the motivation for "revenue-sharing" in the first place.

How about just reducing taxes? And letting the states control their own affairs?

The changes required recipients to register with employment services on a monthly basis in order to receive their welfare checks. The number of welfare recipients declined due to those individuals entering the work-force, enabling them to contribute to the country, their communities, and their families. Other reforms included:

- Requiring recipients to find a job after two years of receiving benefits.

- Placing a limit of five years on benefits paid by federal funds.

- Encouraging two-parent families and discouraging out-of-wedlock births.

- Beefing up enforcement of child support.

- Ending welfare as an entitlement program.

This transition took place during an economic-boom cycle, so jobs were found by most of those who sincerely sought employment.

The present-day case is rather different. In every corner of the country, we are experiencing the worst decline in economic activity since the Great Depression. What is unfortunate is that individuals and entities continue manipulating the system during these difficult times.

Somehow the loopholes in any law—no matter how obscure—will always be found by devious individuals. Something is terribly wrong when you see states paying

$1500 per month per child to a single-parent household. As a result many such recipients continue producing illegitimate children simply to increase their monthly check. Paying taxpayer dollars, based entirely on the number of children recipients have, is sufficient evidence that this government program, whether on the state or federal level, is not fulfilling the original purpose. Instead, it provides an incentive to produce children, and nothing else.

At $1500 per child, an unwed mother of six receives $9000 per month, or $108,000 per year, *tax-free*! And you don't have to be a citizen: illegal aliens can sign up for this gravy-train the same as American citizens. Other benefits accrue as well, as if they were needed. This "entitlement" allows these women to make more money than most single working mothers—or two-parent families, for that matter.

We agree: this is outrageous and an affront to every hard-working taxpayer. One must ask, then: why are the states and the federal government encouraging people to produce children out of wedlock? Is it really their intent to produce a phalanx of fatherless children? Surely those children don't benefit from such an existence.

Let's ask this question: how are Americans affected by federal social programs? Consider for yourself the worthiness of these seemingly charitable programs.

The truth is that the unemployment rates in the poorest American neighborhoods is not the government's stated rate: at this writing, it is closer to 41%. (When an economy is left alone by the government, all segments of society benefit—no less a visionary than John F. Kennedy himself said as much.) The truth is that race-baiting "community organizers" like Al Sharpton, Jesse Jackson, Louis Farrakhan, and Reverend Jeremiah Wright—and even the current President before he was elected to the Illinois legislature—have done less than nothing to promote real human progress within those depressed communities.

The truth is that community organizers are the only individuals who reap any benefit, while the people they claim to help and care about ... *stay poor*. Something is terribly wrong with this picture.

If welfare programs work, and they really improve people's ability to provide for themselves, to become self-sufficient people who pay taxes instead of consuming them, then why is the welfare system growing out of control? Why are many of our cities on the verge of bankruptcy—not to mention the state and federal governments?

Government has been running welfare for more than eighty years. If they really knew what they were doing, poverty would be gone. The War on Poverty would have been won by now. Instead, government is utterly incompetent in this task. The people they claim to care about so much have not benefited at all, but instead remain welfare slaves.

We noticed that "hope and change" disappeared in 2009. Haven't heard a word about them since then. Nothing seems to have changed for the better for the downtrodden. We wonder what they hope for now...

Let's dig a little deeper.

The truth is that pride of ownership is not part of these poor communities (if you don't own your piece of the housing project you live in, why should you take any pride in its upkeep and appearance?). Public housing requires no accountability on the part of the resident. As a result, residents don't appreciate or respect the value of the property because they don't generate the income required to maintain it, let alone own it. Even worse, there is no incentive to fix this problem, nor to rid this part of society of the "entitlement"[2] mentality.

The sad fact remains: many welfare families have reached the fourth or even fifth generation of slavish dependence. Instead of moving toward achieving the American Dream, they are being pushed further and further away *from* it.

This is success? This is an example of public spending achieving its purpose?

---

[2] You'll recall our remark earlier in this book about liberals (progressives) changing the name of things when those things are found out for what they are. Changing the name of "welfare programs" to "entitlements" was at the same time both politically brilliant and a cruel poison pill not only for those "served" by these so-called "entitlements," but for the country as a whole.

> *Vote for me, and I'll set you free! ... Politicians say more taxes will solve everything. And the band played on...*
> **—The Temptations, "Ball of Confusion" (1971)**

And ultimately, supporters of these programs always bring up race. Yet the black-to-white ratio in our prison system is seven-to-one; fifty per cent of blacks drop out of high school; and the black illegitimacy rate is seventy percent.

The truth is that the United States is the only nation that has supported such welfare programs—to the tune of 40,000,000,000,000 (forty trillion) taxpayer dollars—over the last sixty years. Think about that figure for a moment. The American taxpayer has given welfare-recipients of all colors the greatest opportunity in history to exit poverty and achieve true independence. In reality, the percentage who actually escape the welfare trap is dismally low.

And progressives call this success?

The truth is that "community organizers" create a sense of "color" failure, always blaming it on white Americans. But the failure is in the community organizers themselves: if they could lead people, instead of merely agitating them, they might attract genuine followers and voluntary financial support. But that's not how the game is rigged. All Americans hear is that poor communities need more monetary support, and more is never enough.

This is an absurd notion.

What the poor truly need is a dose of reality and some genuine leadership, which would yield a work ethic over time. They would be far better off if the current breed of community organizers became extinct.

"Progressive" welfare policies have not created a better society, and, the Obama administration seems determined not to solve the problem, but to exploit it by deepening and reopening old divides in this country. As a result, the opportunity for genuine reform of these inefficient programs will never be realized, at least during Obama's term.

Food stamps (even though there's a new term for them, the old name is still well entrenched and widely used, as a web search showed, even though the stamps themselves have been replaced by a debit card); Section 8 housing; student loans (and the accompanying grants for many students, which don't have to be repaid); public education; and all the rest continue consuming ever-larger trainloads of the taxpayer's capital, with no chance for the recipients ever to escape poverty in their shortened life-spans. Yes, it's true: people who live on welfare live shorter lives than people who do not.

The "solution" has instead become the problem.

As the number of welfare-recipients grows, the states and the federal government have no choice but to raise taxes, or create more debt (another form of capital-consumption), all to support the snowballing dependent class. Is this not the definition of serfdom?

None Dare Call It Serfdom

In the Middle Ages, the nobility (knights, barons, dukes, and kings) owned land. But more than that, they owned the people who lived on the land and worked it. In exchange for this servitude, the serfs received protection in time of war, and were protected against starvation. If someone took sick and couldn't work as well, they were fed by the feudal lord, and when a hostile force invaded, the serfs took refuge in the feudal lord's castle. To be sure, this paragraph is but a brief description of a complex social system, but aspects of feudalism remain to this day.

And one feudal aspect is returning, like a vampire from the grave...

One critical portion of feudalism was the allegiance to the nobleman ahead of you in the hierarchy. The serf owed allegiance to the knight or baron; the knight or baron to the duke; and when kings were sufficiently strong, the dukes to the king. Any of these aristocrats could summon the group below them and those people had no choice: when the baron called, all of his knights were compelled to answer, as well as all of his serfs.

And in return, the nobleman delivered protection.

Most people, if they have heard of serfdom at all, consider it a form of slavery. The serfs, who worked the land, were compelled to deliver a portion of their crop (whether grain or animals) to the overlord. The ratio was about a third. Raised three pigs? Give one to the baron. Harvested three hundred bushels of wheat? A hundred to the baron. And so on.

In short, serfs could expect to work (in effect) one day in three for the baron and the rest for themselves. And while they couldn't leave the land, most of them were illiterate, so going somewhere else just wasn't one of the choices open to them. Of course, over time, this changed in most of Europe, and the serfs were freed (most of whom became tenant farmers, but that's another topic entirely). The critical piece: serfs paid 33% of their work to the lord, and *all of them* got something in return for that. Something real, something tangible, in return for their in-kind taxes.

If you doubt us, if you think feudalism is dead, we suggest trying either or both of two things: spend some time in uniform and see how well "discussion" with higher authority works out for you, or go to college and see how well arguing with the large majority of professors works out for you. The military and higher education are the last vestiges of feudalism, though, as hinted-at above, one is returning.

Taxpayers now pay far more than 33% of their money to the government. Most end up in the 25% bracket, you say, and that's less than 33%! But that doesn't count state income tax (in those states that have them); it doesn't count state sales tax (it's getting harder and harder to find a sales-tax rate under 8% anywhere). It doesn't include property tax—you think renters don't pay property tax? Be serious: higher property tax is passed to the renter in the form of higher rent. So there's another two or three thousand a year, depending on where you live and other variables.

The Tax Foundation announces each year the exact date of "Tax Freedom Day," meaning the day of the year when Americans are no longer working for the government and are instead working for themselves. It varies from year to year, and in years within your authors' recollection, it has fallen in May quite a few times. In 2016, Tax Freedom Day was April 24th.

Hold the phone!

The Tax Foundation went on to say that *if you include government borrowing*... Tax Freedom Day in 2106 was May 10th.

But wait! There's more!

Your actual Tax Freedom Day varies by state.

In Mississippi, Tax Freedom Day for 2016 was April 5th. In Connecticut, it was May 21st (New Jersey and New York were right behind Connecticut at May 12th and May 11th, respectively).

If you stir all the numbers together, and include government borrowing (which is, after all, a major theme of this book), you worked for the overlords for 130 days. To put it another way, you delivered 35.5% of your work to the overlords (this year is a leap year). But that's better than serfdom, right?

Not at all. Serfs got winters off; nothing grew during that part of the year.

But don't feel so bad. Apparently the economists at

the foundation didn't count Leap Day (February 29th) in their calculations, so this year was one day better than last year. And yes, we're being facetious.

But if you want to, you can choose not to feel bad about this: Tax Freedom Day in the United Kingdom (*aka* Great Britain) in 2015 was May 31st: a full 150 days into the year. And if you count government borrowing, the true Tax Freedom Day for 2015 in the UK was June 29th (180 days into the year, meaning Brits delivered 49.3% of their wealth to their overlords in 2015).

Tax-paying Americans pay more of their productivity to their overlords than medieval serfs, and arguably work more hours when you account for agricultural work's difference from twenty-first-century jobs.

And none dare call it serfdom. Don't you wonder why not?

And many demand we call it "progress." Don't you wonder why?

* * * *

Welfare recipients must be weaned off this toxic burden on society, educated about family values, and the career-politicians that support these "entitlements" must be voted out! This welfare-path, this path the United States has walked for more than eighty years, does not create a prosperous society. Instead, it contributes to societal death, both monetarily and morally. Even more importantly, the individuals being "helped" are harmed monetarily and morally, too. And that unalterable truth should disturb "progressives" greatly, but apparently it doesn't.

You have to ask yourself, are welfare recipients any better off? Have their neighborhoods improved? Of course not. These "benefits" do not motivate recipients to seek opportunity, to exit the poverty, or to contribute to society. Welfare reform—*genuine* reform!—is desperately needed.

Interestingly, the need isn't uniform; the welfare problem is not uniformly distributed throughout the country. States such as California, Illinois, Michigan, and New York have the largest welfare roles, because the Democratic Party has dominated the agenda and have traditionally supported these types of programs as opposed to the more fiscally conservative Republicans.

> *You cannot help the poor by destroying the rich.*
> *You cannot strengthen the weak by weakening the*
> *strong. You cannot bring about prosperity by*
> *discouraging thrift. You cannot lift the wage-*
> *earner up by pulling the wage-earner down. You*
> *cannot further the brotherhood of man by inciting*
> *class hatred. You cannot build character and*
> *courage by taking away people's initiative and*
> *independence. You cannot help people permanently*
> *by doing* for *them, what they could and should do*
> *for themselves.*
>
> —William J. H. Boetcker (1916)

Boetcker's wisdom demonstrates the principles once universally recognized by this great nation. But the "progressives" do not understand (or refuse to see) that fundamental truth. Isn't it ironic that poor people continue to elect Democrats, who in turn keep them poor through welfare programs?

Lest you think we paint with too broad a brush, consider the following examples, which illustrate the grander truth in individual cases. The following top-ten American poverty cities have not elected a Republican mayor—either ever, or in many years.

- Number one: Detroit, MI, which has never elected a Republican Mayor, also has the highest poverty rate in the country.

- Number two: Buffalo, NY. Buffalo has not elected a Republican since 1954.

- Number three: Cincinnati, OH. Cincinnati has not elected a Republican since 1984.

- Number four: Cleveland, OH. No Republican mayor since 1989.

- Number five: Miami FL. Miami has never had a Republican mayor.

- Number six: St. Louis, MO. The last time the Gateway City had a Republican in the mayor's office was 1949.

- Number seven: El Paso, TX. El Paso also has never had a Republican mayor.

- Number eight: Milwaukee, WI. No Republican mayor since 1908.

- Number nine: Philadelphia, PA. No Republican mayor since 1952.

- Number ten: Newark, NJ. Newark has not voted in a Republican mayor since 1907.

There appears to be a pattern here. Could it be that the "progressive" agenda, so popular with voters in these cases (and at the federal level, too) could be the problem, and not the solution? Could it be that destruction of free and open competition, the advent of forced unionism, and the notion that someone else should pay for your troubles in these cities is instead ... destroying not only the cities themselves, but destroying the people who live in them?

And if that's the case, what bodes for the entire United States?

If welfare worked, it would not create such a capital-consuming burden on the working class. If welfare worked, the roles would diminish each year until no more people needed it. If welfare worked, the economy would grow and more and more jobs would be created.

You know better than that.

The poor are poorer; the criminal-justice system is overwhelmed; and life-expectancy for welfare recipients is well below the national average. Drug- and alcohol-abuse runs rampant in this demographic. This unsustainable path, directed by career-politicians and community organizers, who claim to believe they are doing good for the poor, are instead killing them.

And killing the American Dream at the same time.

Eight

And It's Not Just Welfare...

Progressives like "affordable" things. Many of their bills are entitled "The Affordable [Fill in the Blank] Act." The National Affordable Housing Act (1990) is one example. But the king of them all, meaning the biggest lie of them all when it comes to making things "affordable" is The Affordable Care Act, *aka* "Obamacare," *aka* herein "ACA."

You've heard about it already, to be sure. Maybe even until you're sick of hearing about it. Yet another entitlement, paid for with dollars Uncle Sam doesn't have (and we have discussed how that works in previous chapters—meaning it doesn't really work, unless you think having your grandchildren pay the tab is a way to make things work).

But "national health care" has been a liberal-progressive icon for decades. Of course, the examples of Anglophone countries in which nationalized health care is less than what we have been accustomed to in this country abound, even to the point of popular songs alluding to it.

Let's talk terms. First of all, there is no such thing as "health care." It's medical care. That means even the expression "health insurance" is a big, fat lie. It is impossible to "insure" your "health." You can, however, manage the risk that goes with medical costs, and that's where medical insurance comes into play.

The medical-insurance field came into existence during World War II because of government interference in the marketplace (see Chapter Two). Things ran pretty well until agitators managed to get enough people to see that things weren't perfect (ignoring the reality that nothing is this world is perfect—*nothing!*—but boy, does screaming about imperfection get votes!). Of course, promising another dose of something for nothing, along with even more "federal oversight" seems, in retrospect, almost inevitable.

In a particularly pathetic, pandering marketing effort to corral unwilling millennials into buying medical insurance they didn't want, the Obama administration mobilized "pajama boy." This is just one example of what passes for "leadership" in recent years. "Wear pajamas?" "Drink hot chocolate?" Seriously?! Thank God these people were not our "leaders" the day after the Pearl Harbor attack...

Just a side note: when did "tyranny" become known as "federal oversight," and how is that one sounds evil and the other—in many, if not most minds—sounds good?

But think about this: third-party payers (insurance companies) would now be overseen by another third-party payer: Uncle Sam. How could this possibly improve things, given what we have seen of the effects that third-party payers wreak upon the marketplace? (And by "marketplace," we mean all aspects of public life we're discussing in this book, however briefly: Social Security, medical care, education, and everything else.)

Yet many people thought it would. Even some big insurance companies (who have since denounced Obamacare as unworkable) became early supporters. Of course, they might have had different motivations.

Wait a minute: big, big companies getting in bed with the Feds... Where have we heard this before?

In any case, you now have four parties to your medical transaction, whether you like it or not. How in God's green Earth could adding another party to an *already flawed situation* make it *less* flawed?

Nevertheless, along with being Obama's most radical proposal, it is also perhaps his biggest, most massive fraud upon the American taxpayer. Obama's tactics, along with those of his acolytes, used to ram this legislation past the Congress has already been described in numerous volumes. The fraud and corruption in establishing the website has also been described in numerous volumes, magazine articles, etc. (Had Amazon been run that way when it was getting established, no doubt brick-and-mortar stores would still be thriving just as much as in the heyday of "going to the mall" when Reagan was President). And the ensuing it's-a-tax-no-it's-not-a-tax-yes-it-is game defies human logic and common sense.

Wasn't the ACA supposed to provide affordable *medical* care to those who didn't have it? (Although somehow, we have a difficult time recalling people complaining about this problem before 2008; maybe the media helped?) And is the ACA providing that affordable medical care?

You've already heard:

- Insurance premiums went up, often by thousands of dollars a year

- Co-pays for visits went up, often as much as 100% or more

- Medications covered either decreased in number, or the amount paid on behalf of policy-holders went down or both

- In some cases, doctor-patient relationships ended because of this interference

And yet we see, in 2016, bumper-stickers from 2102, proudly proclaiming "Obamacare: Signed, Sealed, and Delivering." The first two are true, one might argue, but exactly what was delivered?

And then we have the corruption of government at the highest levels. Nancy Pelosi, then Speaker of the House, famously proclaimed "We have to pass the bill to find out what's in it."

Why didn't Americans riot and protest? Did Americans fail to understand that *no one who voted for the bill knew what it said*?! Apologists could argue that it's impossible to know everything in a 2,200+-page bill; as far as we are concerned, that's an argument against the current state of affairs, an argument in favor of dismantling half of the federal bureaucracy. (Moreover, the fact that no one who voted for an annual federal budget has known everything that was contained in it, at least since 1993, only reinforces the point.)

And yet... And yet...

After it was passed, as more and more fatal flaws emerged as dutiful bureaucrats "enforced the [new] law," changes were needed. One Size Fits All didn't work (surprise!). So we ask: how many changes did Obama make after the legislation was passed without Congressional approval? Changing laws is, after all, not the President's job, nor has he the authority to do so. That Constitutional power resides in Congress.

And for symbolic purposes, we ask: it cost *how* much to create the ACA website? Hundreds of millions were wasted in corrupt federal-contract awards to incompetent Beltway Bandits. We know: a few hundred million is considered a drop in the bucket in terms of the federal budget.

> *A million here, and a million there, and pretty soon you're talking about real money...*
> —Senator Everett Dirksen

As it turns out, the website-creation contract was not offered out for bids in a "fair and open competition." Michele Obama's roommate from college, Toni Townes-Whitley, senior vice president at CGI Federal, a Canadian multinational company headquartered in Montreal, Quebec was awarded the $678 million no-bid contract to design and implement the ACA Health Care website.

No American companies could do this work? Your authors are free-traders, and NAFTA is a good thing; but no competing bids, and the contract went to a non-American company? Perhaps in their wisdom, your federal care-takers knew no one in the United States was good enough at "tech" to put the thing together.

$678 million? For a website? Granted, we do not claim this was an easy task; software development is a complicated effort, as your authors know from first-hand experience. But a number more like five or ten million dollars seems much more appropriate—especially since the $678 million-dollar product crashed and burned on launch.

George Schindler, the President of CGI Group, became a huge Obama-Democratic donor after the company was awarded the ACA-website contract. $678 million spent to create a bug-ridden website, that needed more truckloads of money to fix, and the Powers That Be claimed, "it's just a short-term fix," "everything is fine?"

And even more specious were claims that the website worked.

How morally wrong is that?

The latest progressive rant is "income inequality." Why does no one hear them saying "political inequality?" Can you help but wonder: were the Obamas handsomely (and discreetly, of course) rewarded for that contract?

Now Democrats are proudly announcing how they will raise more money for the 2016 election than Republicans. Don't you wonder *why*?

Such corrupt behavior in government limits competition, creates inefficiency, and allows the corrupt conspirators to benefit monetarily. Most elected officials retire from Washington wealthy, and with the huge benefits and pensions, all because of political inequality. The end result is more debt, a shrinking middle-class, and the destruction of this republic's very foundation.

Do we overstate the case? Let's let Obama himself answer the question with his own words, when he was pitching his hopey-changey reform to the taxpayers.

- *Obamacare Lie #1:* "If you like your healthcare plan, you'll be able to keep your healthcare plan. Period. No one will take it away. No matter what."

As it turns out, many Americans who were perfectly happy with their existing coverage have simply lost it because of the ACA. According to the Congressional

Budget Office, the increased costs passed on to employers will be unaffordable, causing those employer to drop coverage entirely (or even lay off employees, a polite expression for "fire"). The medical-insurance coverage that millions of Americans had been perfectly happy with was being taken away by Obama's sales-pitch.

- *Obamacare Lie #2:* "Under my plan, no family making less than $250,000 a year will see any form of tax increase."

This is another falsehood. As the program entrenches over the years, its costs increase, which will cause taxes to increase, so the responsible, working, tax-paying American will feel the pain. There is a "mandate tax", a 2.4% tax on medical devices, a 10% tax on tanning services (what in the world have tanning services to do with medical care?!) and a penalty for withdrawing money from your health savings account for non-medical circumstances.

We might add: candidate Obama had no plan. He said he did, but he lied.

- *Obamacare Lie #3:* "I will not sign a plan that adds one dime to our deficits—either now or in the future."

Obama campaigned in part on the notion that adding to the national debt and running a deficit was unpatriotic (among other adjectives). Wise Americans knew he was a liar then. Now the results are in. The Congressional Budget Office recently raised the estimated cost for the

ACA over the next decade from $814 billion to $1.047 trillion. Obama consistently stated that the ACA will *reduce* the budget, when in fact it will not. How can *anyone* believe the lie that spending more will reduce expenditures?!

- *Obamacare Lie #4:* Obamacare will "cut the cost of a typical family's premium by up to $2,500 a year."

For a family of four, the cost in 2012 for the "bronze program" was $15,745. The cost for the same "bronze program" (the cheapest plan) increased to at least $20,000 in 2016. Did you see any savings in your policy? It has been widely reported—and discussed in social media—that millions of Americans that have signed up have seen their deductibles and costs increase since the ACA inception. But it gets even better: in 2016, automobile-insurance premiums skyrocketed. Guess why.

- *Obamacare Lie #5:* "The new healthcare law will improve, not hurt, the quality of American healthcare."

Common sense will tell you that adding 40,000,000 uninsured buyers to an already-saturated market cannot result in improvement. Doing that in any situation forces the quality of anything down. Moreover, how many of those 40,000,000 individuals are not American citizens, and therefore do not pay (direct) taxes?

To make matters worse, numerous skilled practitioners have left medicine. To be sure, estimates vary, but any reasonable person must know that forcing methods upon practitioners of any profession that make doing their work more difficult and even more expensive will drive those practitioners away. The only possible result is large, monolithic, unpleasant medical practices that resemble military medicine, in which medical care is practiced by committee instead of your own doctor.

Maybe that doesn't matter to you now. But trust us: it will someday.

- *Obamacare Lie #6:* "It's not a government takeover: I don't believe that government can or should run health-care."

Mr. Obama, that's a lie on its face. You think government ought to run everything in the marketplace. It is estimated that health-care, prior to federal interference, was 18% of the American economy. If you believe in interventionism, how can anyone believe Obama, and people like him, don't want to take over that private sector of the economy? The Department of Health and Human Services clearly has more power now, since the DC cartel has gotten in bed with the large insurance companies.

- *Obamacare Lie #7:* "The state health insurance exchanges will open on time."

The so-called exchanges that Obama promised were not up and running on time, from the inception. Many states opted out of establishing them at all, passing the costs back to Uncle Sam (which means the taxpayers!).

Data-population, when individuals could log on at all, was often incorrect. Numerous crashes and other errors on the state exchanges caused many Americans not to sign up at all (which yielded a tax penalty for them!—but remember, "it's not a tax"...).

Even the believers now realize the lies that were told to the American people to get this unaffordable bill passed. Even some big insurance companies have finally admitted the fiduciary truth: the magic system proposed by the junior senator from Illinois in 2008 is just so much smoke and mirrors. But it got him elected...

Twice.

The progressives—liberals, socialists, interventionists, whatever you wish to call them, because they are all one and the same—have been creating and perpetuating debt-ridden "programs" for eight years. These panaceas for whatever ailed us at the time do not, and have not, allowed the free market to work. This federal behemoth, the ACA, was a disaster from its inception, a calamity waiting to happen. It is nothing more than a debt-ridden, corrupt government take-over of the greatest medical system on Earth.

Everything progressives have legislated has added to the debt. There is scarcely a single "social program" in DC that is funded by the Americans benefiting from it. Government has simply gotten too big, too intrusive, overrun with layers and layers of inefficient bureaucracy. These government "programs" staffed by government employees don't solve any of society's problems—they create more problems instead, in spite of the best intentions some of them hold.

And yet... The underlying causes of these government failures are never discussed.

Why not?

Nine

Social Security, the Ultimate Ponzi Scheme

Social Security's roots lie in nineteenth-century Germany. Otto von Bismarck, in his role as chancellor, made a compromise with the Social Democrats for two reasons: to further his agenda, and to take the wind out of the sails of the Social Democrats' agenda, which was, until the late *twentieth* century, the overthrow of the government. Violently, if need be. Needless to say, Bismarck's agenda found itself at odds with the Social Democrats' agenda.

But the idea caught on, and American excitement over things German in the late nineteenth century (for example, new methods in higher education) allowed the seeds to germinate. And for the record, the Germans called them "old-age pensions."

One-sentence version: Bismarck agreed to the idea in order to prevent anti-government violence. But he got as much as he gave, at least until he was ousted as chancellor by Kaiser Wilhelm II.

Fast-forward to 1933. The United States, and most of the industrial world, found itself in the throes of the Great Depression. Franklin Delano Roosevelt, with a compliant Congress, proposed a new (to Americans, sort of) thing he called Social Security. Regardless of what you think of it, the name was a stroke of marketing genius.

The plan was pitched to Americans as an "insurance policy." The law was written such that the Social Security number would never be used as an identification number (there were people afraid of federal over-reach even before George Orwell wrote his famous book, *1984*).

So much for *that* plan...

One more thing: why was the retirement age set at 65? Several reasons have been suggested, and all those reasons probably have something to do with it. For example, many, if not most, Americans in 1933 didn't expect to live to 65, or if they did, not much past it. But one single factor stands out: the German old-age-pension law made retirement mandatory at 65. Why?

Because Bismarck, who got himself exempted from the law, was able to clean out his political opponents who were already beyond 65...

You wouldn't let your children take candy from the friendly stranger in the black sedan. Why do you expect virtuous things of people who promise you something for nothing?

* * * *

President Franklin Delano Roosevelt pressed ambitiously for legislation that resulted in the Social Security Act of 1935. For the first time, Americans were required to pay taxes for, theoretically, their old age. The law was passed in August, 1935.

Immediate payouts were authorized to the states. You might say this was originally a federal program to fund state activities, or at least so it seemed on the surface. Congress included in the Social Security Act aid for the blind and aged, as well as orphaned children and needy women.

Before proceeding, it should be mentioned that this program was pitched to Americans as an insurance policy: another common expression for Social Security used to be "old-age insurance." In short, taxpayers (or at least many of them) saw the new law as a mandatory insurance policy.

That should make you nervous all by itself.

Of course, such vote-getting legislation required a new tax. And of course, this example had what is euphemistically called a "phased-in" tax. We say "euphemistically" because that's a word "progressives" like that really means "financial time bomb."

Here's how it worked out in 1935.

- For the year 1935: no taxes collected

- For the year 1936: no taxes collected

See how this works? Taxes didn't begin until January, 1937: right after the Presidential (and, of course, Congressional) elections. Remind you of anything you might have heard about our magic medical-insurance in the last few years? Just kick the can down the road...

In short, recipients got paid for almost a year and a half before any American paid taxes to support those payments. That means there was no wealth behind this so-called "insurance." (Bear in mind that the employer's share was called an "excise tax" in the original legislation, which is a far cry from an "insurance premium.")

It gets better.

- For the years 1937-1942, inclusive: 1 per cent of wages

- For the years 1943-1948, inclusive: 2 per cent of wages

- Starting in 1949, and forever after: 3 per cent of wages

Even FDR couldn't have imagined he'd be President that long, and one doubts he had any vision in 1935 of being President past 1940. A critical provision stated that the Social Security tax would *not* be allowed as a deduction for employees against their income tax. No shock results from noting that that provision hasn't changed.

For employers, the hit was slightly different: though the rate was exactly the same, the employer's payment was considered an excise tax and not exempted as a deduction from the employer's income tax. The words "excise tax" are critical here: there was never any attempt to disguise what the new system was, at least to employers.

None of this was ever voluntary, though there were interesting exemptions that no longer apply—for example, agricultural, casual, and domestic laborers (think there might have been some cheating there?) as well as federal employees. Other special groups were exempted who remain exempted—for example, railroad workers, state employees, and for work performed outside the United States.

A key figure in the legislation was $3,000 of annual wages ($250 per month). In 1935, that was a lot of money. If that employee made exactly $3,000 in 1937, and if inflation never happened and his wages never went up, he could look forward to a monthly payment of fifteen dollars.

That's right: $15.

All in return for a monthly tax of $2.50. Of course, by 1949, if that employee was young enough, he'd be paying $7.50 per month in Social Security tax.

People aged 65 and older in 1935 never paid any of these taxes. Hence the (quite correct) assertion that they got a free ride. There was never any wealth behind the Social Security System. It was all robbing Peter to pay Paul.

Of course, the excesses in the trust fund could be invested, but only in United States securities. Innocuous and safe on the surface to be sure. But the interest on those "investments," of course, come from taxes paid by ... taxpayers!

Obviously, no one has been talking about any excesses

in the Social Security "trust fund" for decades. In fact, the "trust fund" was scrapped during the Johnson administration as part of LBJ's "Great Society."

The ultimate Ponzi scheme.

And, of course, eighty-one years later after taxpayers have been fleeced their entire working lives by this financial fiasco, the ultimate political lightning rod. Never in history has any government largess screamed louder for reform than this one. And never in history has any "program" been so unassailable.

How can you escape the conclusion that FDR was buying re-election for himself and his party in 1936, the New Deal having done nothing whatsoever to end the Great Depression? To be sure, there had been tiny improvements here and there, but nothing like "recovery." And in 1937, another economic crash occurred, leaving Americans just as badly off as they had been in 1931.

Spending a country's way to prosperity is a cruel joke, and an outright lie.

Nowadays, of course, with the inflation of the last eight decades behind us, the tax is at 7.65% of the first $90,000. And during the Carter administration, illegal immigrants became eligible for payments from a system into which they had paid, theoretically, not one thin dime.

But at least the Social Security payments ("benefits") were tax-free.

They were tax-free, at any rate, until Congress began taxing them in the early 1980s. And at least that was partial taxation for awhile. But now, Social Security payments are effectively fully taxable as ... income!

Wasn't this supposed to be an "insurance program?"

We won't get into the numerous ways that payments can be reduced. Not only is the math painful, but we haven't the space.

But it might still not be so bad, had the Johnson administration not layered over medical payments in the 1960s (again, part of the Great Society legislation) onto the Social Security System (old-age insurance!). A sure-fire way to bankrupt an already horribly flawed, corrupt system even sooner.

A Real-World Ponzi Scheme (Where the Swindlers Got Punished)

The late, great newsman and commentator, Paul Harvey, used to intone frequently that if any insurance company managed their policies the way Social Security was run, the state regulators would shut them down instantly. The clear message was this: government ought not to be in the insurance business because it was inept and incompetent to do so. Their role, at the state level, was suited to insurance-regulation, not insurance-administration. And certainly not engaging in the business of *providing* insurance.

He also used to say, and rightly so, that Social Security was a Ponzi Scheme.

About thirty-five years ago, as of this writing, one of

your authors encountered a real-life Ponzi scheme. Times were tough, money was tight, inflation was high, and interest rates were higher. People moaned and groaned that The American Dream was a thing of the past.

Out-of-town operators showed up and the word got out quickly: bring in a thousand dollars, and in a few days, you'll have $16,000! Tax-free! What could be better?

Bear in mind, you could buy half a decent house in 1980 for $16,000, at least in most parts of the country.

All you had to do... Was bring in more people. That, and make a "gift" of your thousand dollars to whomever brought *you* in. It was a bonanza! Think how many times you could turn $1,000 into $16,000! Your money problems would be over in a week!

One of your authors knew a couple guys who were simply *aching* to dive in. And maybe twice—because there was no limit to how many times you could enter into the "gift program." Elaborate parties were thrown—sort of the disco-era equivalent of "raves"—in which the arrangements were made and the "gifts" were exchanged.

You probably already know the flaw in the plan: there aren't enough people to make the scheme work forever. Start with two, and multiply it by itself. Then do that ten times. Now multiply that number by the number of suckers all trying to do the same thing. In short, the ones who get in early—real early—make out like bandits. Literally and figuratively. And the johnny-come-latelys get fleeced.

Why would any thinking person do this?

You wouldn't. And your author's friends saw the light, and both kept their thousand dollars. And after a couple weeks, what used to be called the "bunco squad" from the local police department shut down the activity, and several arrests were made.

These scam-artists *had committed crimes!*

And why do you care?

Because this is *exactly* how Social Security works, including how it was designed from the outset. The people who got paid in 1935 never put in a single dime. They got something for nothing, at the expense of their children. And their neighbor's children. And, in a few years, their neighbor's ***grand***children...

And the can kept getting kicked down the road.

Who would sign up for such a thing? An "insurance policy" that insured nothing, had no accumulated wealth behind it, and had no real oversight? What thinking person would do that? Why did you?

Because you were *forced* to...

Ten

Leadership?

Americans talk about their elected officials in a number of ways. One word that gets dropped from time to time is "leader." Or, sometimes a candidate touts his or her "leadership." Both terms are the sort of word that defies definition, at least to some degree. But most people would agree that they know leaders when they see them.

Sadly, many so-called leaders are just charlatans blessed with charisma. Like the Pied Piper in the fairy tale, who got children to follow him to their doom (check the original story if you doubt us), many of our elected "leaders" are taking us in the wrong direction—even those of us who don't want to go, even though we know we don't want to go.

But we also have a problem that has plagued us since the New Deal: appointed officials of all ranks who have the power to write regulations that carry the force of law.

How many Environmental Protection Agency (EPA) bureaucrats did *you* elect? Yet they write regulations that affect you directly, and you can be put in jail if you don't follow them. Yet you can't vote them out of office.

This is self-government?

This problem, which we have used the EPA to illustrate, relates to every facet of American life, including the banking and mortgage problems we discuss in detail elsewhere in this book. The notion of dictatorial control by our government is a pox on self-government and personal liberty —a curse on the American Dream——yet we continue voting these people into office (the ones we *can* vote for, that is).

Not all government officials behave this way, to be sure, but far too many of them do. If you want to figure out which way your elected officials lean, find out their thoughts on appointing "czars" to solve this or that particular problem. Then you'll know what to do.

Some have called the current President the first American Emperor. Historians will decide whether that's true. Our purpose in bringing this up is that the root word of "President" is "preside." "To preside" means to "to occupy the place of authority or control, as in an assembly or meeting." It does *not* mean "to rule," "to reign," or "to dictate." And the meeting in the definition implies taxpayers as the assembled.

A proper President leads. A proper President therefore must set good examples. And yet in the last seven years, Americans have watched more battalions of bureaucrats file into Washington, DC to write more and more regulations.

But those bureaucrats took an oath of poverty in order to raise their moral standard so high that they could justify their metaphorical preaching to the rest of us, right? Yeah, right. Sure they did...

Let's examine the wasteful bureaucracies that have been supported by both sides of the aisle for decades. They have done nothing positive for the country, but have instead created an ever-larger, increasingly inefficient government. If these bureaucracies where efficient, America would not be $20,000,000,000,000 in debt. It is as simple as that. We don't care how much money the Federal Reserve prints: we will not get out of this financial disaster until the interventionists are voted out and the elites discussed in this book are disbanded or disenfranchised.

The failure should have happened in 2008. Instead the interventionists have prolonged the failure, without any accountability, none-of them imprisoned or fined as "Boss" Tweed was for his malfeasance, nor even identified as the cause of America's financial collapse. How do we turn this speeding battleship around and set a positive course for the backbone of America, the middle class?

Finding and electing leaders is a start. Since the President is supposed to lead, let's consider just a single facet of his leadership. Surely, if he has been a good and proper President, he has led by example. One such example would be his appointees, and more importantly, their salaries.

We realize these salaries, compared to the total federal expenditures, are a grain of sand on the beach. But the importance lies in the example they set, and in the tone they set for the rest of government to follow.

The raises awarded by the Obama White House for the following employees during this economic crisis shows us just how out of touch President Obama and his administration are when it comes to increasing debt, spending money, and placing the burden on the taxpayer.

This type of behavior could not be justified if anyone in Washington had the slightest clue about economics and how destructive debt is on the country.

Some of these government employees received an 86% increase in salary after having only been on the job for two years. Does that happen in the private sector? We wonder how older Americans react when they have no cost-of-living increase and then see the generous pay raises for Obama's minions. Do these people contribute anything? Are they critical to the support of this administration in these dire times? These positions could be terminated tomorrow, and the American government would still function, and not one soul would notice.

And while some have since gone on to other things, they have been replaced by other of their ilk. What is important is to consider these examples and to use them to evaluate the leadership practiced over the last seven years.

- Matt Vogel, Special Asst. to the Pres. for Economic Policy: $71,400 to $130,500 (an increase of **83%** = $59,100).

- Heather Zichal, Deputy Asst. to the Pres. for Energy and Climate Change: $100,000 to $140,000 (an increase of **40%** = $40,000).

- Kevin Lewis, Director of African-American Media: $42,000 to $78,000 (an increase of **86%** = $36,000).

- Elizabeth Olsen, Special Asst. Director of Presidential Correspondence: $76,500 to $110,000 (an increase of **44%** = $33,000).

- Jessica Wright, Deputy Asst. to the Pres. and Director of Scheduling: $96,000 to $130,000 (an increase of **34%** = $33,100).

- Lauren Paige, Special Asst. to the Pres. and Director of Message Planning: $62,000 to $95,000 (an increase of **53%** = $33,000).

- Elizabeth Nelson, Deputy Director of Scheduling: $45,900 to $75,000 (an increase of **63%** = $29,100).

- Ashley Tate-Gilmore, Director of Travel Office: $45,900 to $75,000 (an increase of **63%** = $29,100).

- Carlos Monje Jr., Spec. Asst. to the Pres. and Chief of Staff of the Domestic Policy Council: $91,800 to $120,000 (an increase of **31%** = $28,000).

- David Cusack, Deputy Asst. to the Pres. and Director of Advance and Operations: $102,000 to $130,000 (an increase of **27%** = $28,000).

- Kimberley Harris, Deputy Asst. to the Pres. and Deputy Council to the Pres.: $130,500 to $158,500 (an increase of **21%** = $28,000).

- Jonathan Samuels, Deputy Asst. to the Pres.: $130,500 to $158,500 (an increase of **21%** = $28,000).

- Thomas Vietor, Senior Director and National Security Staff Spokesman: $78,000 to $105,000 (an increase of **35%** = $27,000).

- Frederico Gardaphe, Deputy Director: $50,000 to $75,000 (an increase of **50%** = $25,000).

- Denis McDonough, Asst. to the Pres. and National Security Advisor: $147,500 to $172,200 (an increase of **17%** = $24,700).

- Johanna Maska, Deputy Director of Advance and Director of Press Advance: $56,100, to $80,000 (an increase of **43%** = $23,900).

- Kwesi Cobbina, Chief of Staff, Office of Legislative Affairs: $42,000 to $65,000 (an increase of **55%** = $23,000).

- Semonti Stephens, Deputy Communications Director: $53,550 to $75,000 (an increase of **40%** = $21,450).

- Amanda Anderson, Senior Legislative Affairs Adviser: $60,000 to $80,000 (an increase of **33%** = $20,000).

- Stacy Koo, Deputy Chief of Staff for Presidential Personnel: $55,000 to $75,000 (an increase of **36%** = $20,000).

- Andrea Turk, Director of Information Services: $50,000 to $70,000 (an increase of **40%** = $20,000).

What do you think these people do to justify as much as an 86% increase in salary? Some of the job-titles alone make us want to see the accompanying position descriptions. Obama's staff is full of numerous assistants to the assistants who do nothing.

Are all these positions necessary? But more importantly, are these examples of how to behave for leaders in government when the country is sinking deeper and deeper into an ocean of debt? Why don't Americans protest this "leadership?"

DC is out of control. Vote the corrupt "leaders" out in 2016.

Eleven

Is There Nothing We Can Do?

All of the economic misery we have discussed in previous chapters has been caused by the powerful alliance between career politicians, the Federal Reserve, and the connected institutions. No one has been held accountable for this economic turmoil, and no one has been prosecuted for corruption or abuse of power, nor for insider-trading. Tax-paying Americans have been compelled to sit back and watch their dollars shrivel in value because this corrupt network of charlatans, instead of doing their jobs and performing competently and ethically, lies to us and deceives us for one reason and one reason only: to support their capital-consuming agenda in order to make themselves rich. And not making themselves rich by growth or wealth-creation as a Carnegie or a Rockefeller would have done, but by robbing taxpayers to pay ... themselves.

American prosperity cannot return, nor can a free-market economy be restored, unless and until this corrupt network is dismantled and held accountable for its actions.

We do know this: the money presses around the world are running 24/7; this cannot continue indefinitely. The world's economies have ceased their historically dynamic behavior, substituting corruption, entitlements, and interference while their citizens become poorer. And while the central banks within these countries continue printing money to bail out the elites that have caused the collapse, the band plays on as if they were the band aboard the *Titanic*.

Perhaps the corrupt see this moment as their last opportunity to pillage and plunder before the inevitable crash. For if the corrupt have the capital beforehand, they will have the funds to start all over again, building new elites once any economic collapse occurs.

America should have been——and would have been——coming out of the recession by now had free-market policies been instituted. Instead, we teeter on the verge of the failure that was postponed via the 2008-09 bail-outs. Far better that the failure had not been postponed: such genuine failure would have cleansed America's economy of the corrupt that have been in control for decades. Instead, the interventionists bailed out the interventionists; that is, they stole from you to bail themselves out.

It has been said that nothing succeeds like success. But these liars have sold us a bill of goods: on their watch, nothing has succeeded like their own failure.

> *"The more they get, the more they need. And every time they get harder and harder to please..."*
>
> —Ray Davies and The Kinks
> "Give the People What They Want" (1981)

What has President Obama continually stated? That the government needs more tax revenue——a weak euphemism for higher taxes. The United States does *not* have a revenue problem; the United States has a *spending* problem. The spending problem is a result of government intervention not just over the last ten years, but over the last eighty years, and the accompanying capital-consuming agenda the "progressive" elites have demanded for more than 100 years.

Why is it that when Louis XVI (the one who lost his head to the guillotine during the French Revolution) is depicted in movies and books, he's evil for wanting more taxes, but "progressives" are hailed as saviors for demanding not only the same thing, but at a higher rate than anything Louis could have dreamed possible?

Either taxpayers demand reform, ending all government economic intervention, or Americans can plan on still-higher tax rates (as in Western Europe) and unvarnished socialism—perhaps even a total collapse of the monetary system as took place in Germany in the 1920s. If such reforms are not enacted after the 2016 elections, American career-politicians will continue spending, printing money, and controlling our everyday lives. Can you envision Greece and Spain on an American scale? Eventually, that will happen unless something changes.

Real change. Not hope-changey charlatan lies.

> *Power tends to corrupt and absolute power corrupts absolutely. Great men are almost always bad men, even when they exercise influence and not authority; still more when you [add] the tendency of the certainty of corruption by authority.*
>
> *Liberty consists in the division of power. [Totalitarianism and tyranny consists], in concentration of power.*
>
> **—Lord Acton**

Lord Acton, the nineteenth-century historian whose famous assessment of power was so popular among the Left during the Vietnam and Watergate eras, doesn't seem to get as much "press" in our universities in the new millennium. Maybe liberty is at odds with progressivism...

When governments claim they must intervene more in an economy, the reality is that past decisions to intervene (interfere) in the economy have not produced the promised results and have instead made things worse. But then the lies continue, and the claim is made that more intervention is needed in order to correct the mistakes from the beginning.

Better that they had kept their hands out of the pie in the first place.

Government has become too big and too powerful for it to resist interfering in markets. The federal government has infiltrated every aspect of our economy.

The only free markets left, aside from black markets, are the farmers markets or flea markets found throughout the country (and some of those are, at least in theory, watched over by state governments, lest a single penny of sales tax escape its clutches).

Even Internet commerce is slowly being taxed, such that sales tax is levied on things that are not normally taxable in a face-to-face transaction at a brick-and-mortar store (delivery charges, for example).

What should tax-paying Americans demand of their elected representatives? First: adherence to the Constitution, not a desire to "work around it." Second: a desire to reform the mess that Washington has made over the last ten decades. Third: a realization that not all business is bad, and that corruption hurts taxpayers.

And maybe, just maybe a fourth thing: a desire to reduce the power of the executive branch. If reducing the power of the executive branch was good enough for the country in the 1970s (after the Johnson and Nixon administrations), then it's good enough for the current crop of clowns holding down the chairs of power at this writing.

DC is so out of touch with the problems facing tax-paying Americans that a thorough house-cleaning is in order. So add a fifth thing to the list: call things for what they are, and stop spending so much damned money! The old saying goes: you have to give to get. America has too many getters and the givers can no longer support them; it's time for a change.

Real change, not hopey-changey smoke-and-mirrors change.

How about these as suggestions? End the War on Drugs. It's a colossal failure and less successful than Prohibition (which was, by the way, a Progressive agenda-item). Want another one? End the Head Start Program, another colossal failure supposedly aimed at making inroads into poor children's performance in schools, which recently was demonstrated to have made ... zero impact in the last fifty years. Yes. Zero impact.

More, you say? Are we still at the "moral equivalent of war" on the "energy crisis?" (The crisis that never existed, we might add.) If so, most of the Department of Energy could go away and most likely no one would notice.

Except taxpayers, of course.

And since the erstwhile Kennedy-era Health, Education, and Welfare Department was split into two such that Education stood on its own... How about an honest assessment of their performance and expenditures? Don't taxpayers deserve an audit of their un-elected—yes, we said what we meant: *un-elected*—bureaucrats have done with their money for more than half a century?

But if that's too difficult a task... Maybe we should just return education to where it was six decades ago: in the hands of the individual states. And not with any revenue-sharing foolishness to go with it.

Americans can no longer bleed money for the

interventionists and their agenda of printing worth-less [*sic*] money, higher taxes, and sky-rocketing debt. The time has come to clean house, and vote in real leaders, not more career-politicians who want to keep on with the same old, same old.

The downfall of civilizations as far back as the Romans began with welfare, economic interference, and corruption. The American system is broken and it is up to the voting public (the part that believes in liberty, free markets, and the Constitution, at any rate) to vote in the genuine leaders who believe in these principles so that the damage can be fixed.

Before things get worse...

Here are some other ideas that have been proposed in the past, but have fallen by the wayside in the last twenty years:

Term Limits

- House members shall be limited to two two-year terms in their lifetime

- Senate members shall be limited to two six-year terms in their lifetime

- House members who have served two terms may only serve one term in the Senate

- Senate members who have served two terms may not serve in the House

Exclusionary Laws

- Congress shall pass no laws that treat the President, members of Congress or any other group of federal employees differently than all other citizens of the United States.

- The President, members of Congress and other Presidential appointees shall receive no pension benefits of any kind other than Social Security during their service to the United States.

Balanced Budget Amendment

- The President shall not submit and Congress shall not pass any budget which contains deficit spending (surplus revenue shall be allowed if and only if used to pay off the national debt).

- In time of war declared by Congress, a deficit may be run to support the war effort; once the war has been declared finished by Congress the accumulated deficit must be repaid in equal amounts over a twenty-year period.

- The national debt, at the time of the adoption of this amendment, shall be repaid in equal installments over a forty-year period.

A Really Radical Idea

- Every new spending bill must be matched by the repeal of an old spending bill at least as large as the one being passed. If Uncle Sam wants $100,000,000 of new spending on X, then Uncle Sam must first repeal spending on Y totaling at least $100,000,000.

Some Not-So-Radical Ideas

- Repeal one law every month for ten years. Trust us: you won't notice. But the budget will. If it's a good-enough idea for base closure and realignment, it's good enough for laws that have outlived their usefulness.

- Reduce the size of the federal work-force (the part that is *not* defense-related, for a change) by 1% a year for five years.

- Close down one cabinet-level department without rolling the jobs into a different cabinet-level department. If that's too hard, close one down by rolling it into a surviving department, but cut the number of jobs in the smaller department.

- Reform Social Security!!!

And we bet that you can think of some good ideas, too. Maybe your local officials or your Congressional people ought to hear about them. Maybe you'll tell them about the ideas we've presented above, too.

If tax-paying Americans don't vote for real change in the 2016 elections, we're only kicking the can down the road. But we can't play kick-the-can forever. The ultimate destination on our current path is a socialistic tyranny in which hard work is punished and equal opportunity will live only in our memories as a fantasy.

But it won't stop at the 2016 elections, or any election cycle, ever. The price of freedom is constant vigilance, and that observation is not limited to military preparedness. Demand real, honest, genuine reform.

Please start today. The country needs you; the Constitution needs you. If you do nothing to put an end to crime and corruption, who will? If you won't stand up and be counted, what will become of the Republic? What will become of freedom and personal liberty?

If not you, then who?

Epilogue

Anytown, USA: Today

The younger man looked at his father closely.

"So the more things change, the more they stay the same."

"Where'd you hear that one, son?"

The younger man smiled.

"You already know that, Dad."

"Just so long as you know I didn't make it up. I just borrowed it."

The father smiled. To his mind, the wheel had finally completed a full cycle. His memory flashed for an instant on the conversation he'd had with his own father not that long ago—or so it seemed to him.

"I know where you got it, Dad. You've been quoting that French proverb for years. But I still can't see how today's political environment is all that similar to how it was when you were my age. Or especially how it was in Grandpa's time."

"Any particular part?"

"Monetary policy…"

The older man laughed, and the son's face twisted into a scowl.

"Son, monetary-policy fights are as old as the Republic. If we can call the country a republic anymore."

The son's face untwisted as he discerned the reason for his father's laughter.

"And that's the second question I have. I'm almost afraid to mention it."

"About the nature of the Republic?"

"Yeah..."

"How about we talk about both of those, if you want. Unless there's more?"

The son looked down at the floor, just for an instant.

"Isn't that enough?" the younger man asked. "It seems everything's going to hell in a hand-basket."

The father smiled at hearing his son use his own grandfather's expression. Apparently some old expressions still resonated.

"So what's on your mind, son?"

"There aren't any leaders anymore. And no public servants. Just greedy people out for themselves, and they pass the bill to the working people who pay taxes. Like that song I used to hear you listening to when I was little: 'The more they get, the more they need, and every time they get harder and harder to please...'"

The older man smiled, nodding as he listened. He imagined easily why his son wanted to keep his thoughts to himself; such thoughts wouldn't have been any more popular in a college classroom in 1986, let alone in the rarefied air-of-no-debate-anywhere found in 2016.

"I think you could find a small number of leaders, if you looked hard enough."

"OK, Dad. I see your point. But you see mine, too. I can see it in your face."

"And you want to know what you can do about it..."

"Yeah, Dad. I do. Things have never been perfect, but the country's on the wrong path. I can do the math: Social Security is a fiscal joke; every year the federal government spends more than it has; and no one seems to want to do anything about it. And for all the money they throw at things, no problem ever gets fixed. If anything, the problems get worse."

The father rethought his son's decision to minor in political science, almost ten years earlier. Perhaps it hadn't been such a bad idea after all.

"And you feel powerless. Maybe even like a pawn?"

"Yeah, Dad. And we're supposed to be practicing self-government?

"You probably don't remember Paul Harvey. He used to say, over and over in his editorial pieces, that self-government without self-discipline can't work. Or words to that effect."

This time, the son nodded as he listened.

"And you want to do something about it?"

The son nodded his answer.

"You may have heard me talk about this before. We have elected a mass of panacea-promising charlatans."

"Sometimes you use harsher words," the son interjected, a gleam in his eye.

"And so I do... But still, you know what I'm driving at."

The son again nodded his concurrence.

"The country has lost the wisdom, it seems, that there is no such thing as something for nothing. Too many people think the government actually has money, without realizing that taxpayers have to pony up all the money the government will ever have. Money is just units of exchange to transfer wealth from one party to another..."

"You'd be surprised how many of my peers simply don't get that, Dad. And forget even younger people."

"Mine, too, son... Mine, too. Anyway... There is *one* thing left that you can do."

"What's that?"

"Find candidates with character. Character is hard to define, but you know it when you see it. They're out there. Find them, and get them to run for office. And get them elected. It's..."

"... a lot of work," the son finished for his father.

"Self-government isn't easy, son. Do you want to secure the blessings of liberty for yourself and your posterity?"

The son smiled.

"You come up with those words by yourself, Dad?"

The father chuckled.

"You know better... But more importantly... Do you want the blessings of liberty? Not only for yourself and your wife, but for your little girl in the other room?"

"Yeah... I do. You *know* I do... I'm tired of those ... people ... in Washington acting like they know everything. I'm past the point where I need to be told what to do all the time, and besides: that was your and Mom's job. Not theirs."

"I guess you have your work cut out for you, then, son."

"But how did it get like this?"

"Teddy Roosevelt said it: comparison is the thief of joy. Except now we have a whole political class that does nothing but create and exploit envy. That's only part of the answer, though," the father replied.

"And I've been wondering for years," the older man went on, "How the Left managed to cobble a coalition of people who simply point fingers and call names, setting group against group, tearing the country to pieces. Unifying nothing. We have to toss these charlatans out of office, or they'll keep at it until there won't be anything left of our America. We'll just be a bigger Yugoslavia, if something doesn't change."

The son's young daughter walked into the room at that moment.

"Grandpa?"

"Yes, sweetheart?"

"Can I sit with you?"

"Of course, precious girl."

The little girl clambered up onto the older man's lap, then leaned in against his chest.

"Grandpa?" she asked.

"Yes, sweetheart?"

"What's Yugoslavia?"

Both men laughed softly.

"My point exactly," the older man said so quietly that his words barely rose above a whisper.

"When you're old enough for school, I'll tell you all about it..."

ABOUT THE AUTHORS

Mike Crane graduated from California State University, Fresno with BA and MA degrees, and completed PhD work at the University of Idaho. Subsequently he worked for the US Navy and finally at the US Air Force Academy, where he taught history in addition to other duties. While at the Air Force Academy, he received the Outstanding Academy Educator Award. Crane was also a member of the 82nd Airborne Division, in which he served as an airborne infantryman.

Matt Grubesic holds a degree in economics from the University of Colorado, and is a proponent of the Austrian school of economics. A long-time entrepreneur, Grubesic is a veteran of the no-holds-barred trading pits, in a time when there were no bailouts and mistakes could cost you your shirt, or a lot more.

Visit
www.mikecraneauthor.com

www.ingramcontent.com/pod-product-compliance
Lightning Source LLC
Chambersburg PA
CBHW070239190526

45169CB00001B/228